The Covenant Never Revoked

*Biblical Reflections on
Christian-Jewish Dialogue*

by
Norbert Lohfink, S.J.

TRANSLATED BY JOHN J. SCULLION, S.J.

PAULIST PRESS
New York/Mahwah, N.J.

Originally published as *Der Niemals Gekündigte Bund* by Verlag Herder Freiburg im Breisgau 1989. English translation copyright © 1991 by The Missionary Society of St. Paul the Apostle in the State of New York.

Library of Congress Cataloging-in-Publication Data

Lohfink, Norbert.
    [Der niemals gekündigte Bund. English]
    The covenant never revoked : biblical reflections on Christian-Jewish dialogue / by Norbert Lohfink ; translated by John J. Scullion.
       p. cm.
    Translation of: Der niemals gekündigte Bund.
    ISBN 0-8091-3228-1
    1. Covenants—Biblical teaching. 2. Bible—Criticism, interpretation, etc. 3. Christianity and other religions—Judaism. 4. Judaism—Relations—Christianity. 5. Judaism (Christian theology) 6. Bible. N.T.—Relation to the Old Testament.
    I. Title.
    BS680.C67L64   1991
    231.7'6—dc20   90-26198
                                               CIP

Published by Paulist Press
997 Macarthur Boulevard
Mahwah, New Jersey 07430

Printed and bound in the
United States of America

Contents

iii

Translator's Foreword

It has been a pleasure to translate *Der niemals gekündigte Bund* by Norbert Lohfink, fellow Jesuit, and colleague and friend for more than thirty years. My only regret is that I have not reproduced in English the eloquence of his fine German.

I agree substantially with the contents of the book. For any mistranslation or misrepresentation, I am entirely to blame.

My thanks are due to Herder & Herder, Freiburg im B., and Paulist Press, N.J., for their ready acceptance of the translation.

John J. Scullion S.J.
Newman College
(University of Melbourne)
Parkville

United Faculty of Theology
Melbourne 3052

Author's Foreword

My book *The Jewishness in Christianity (Das Jüdische am Christentum)* appeared in early 1987. It was not intended as a contribution to Jewish-Christian dialogue. It was to be an examination of the Christian conscience. Any theological statement on the relationship between Jews and Christians was at most marginal. Nevertheless, the result was that I was invited on many occasions to dialogues, lectures, and discussions on the theme "Jews and Christians."

After an animated talk with an exegetical colleague I composed an article in which I presented my views. I gave it the form of an imaginary interview. I offered it to journals and radio stations. But the theme appeared to be too unwelcome. Nobody wanted it.

I developed everything somewhat further when I was invited by the Sisters of Our Lady of Zion to take part in a theological seminar of the congregation in Rome, January 3–7, 1989, together with Rabbi Norman Solomon of Birmingham. The result was an introductory presentation on the theme, "The Covenant Never Revoked." I thank Sister Katherine Wolff of the general council of the congregation and especially the superior general, Sister Patricia Watson, for the invitation and the opportunity to take part in the subsequent discussions. I learned much there from the sisters and the rabbi and later reworked the German text of my presentation once more. Hence this small contribution. The publishing house of Herder was prepared to publish it at once. For this I am grateful. I thank Georg Braulik, Wolfgang Fenneberg, and Hans-Winfried Jüngling, who all read the manuscript at different stages and made many helpful comments.

I hope that the text may be of assistance to some readers. One should expect neither a complete exegesis of the biblical passages nor a systematic treatment (which would in no way be concentrated on the key word "covenant"). Whoever wants a thorough discussion of the New Testament passages treated is referred to the first part of Erich Grässer, *Der alte Bund im Neuen. Exegetische Studien zur Israelfrage im Neuen Testament,* WUNT 35, Tübingen, 1985, pp. 1–134. There is also a detailed bibliography. At crucial points Erich Grässer lays different emphases than the present book. When in many places he develops theses which are the result of the conviction of an "individual principle of salvation" introduced into the history of revelation with Christ, I can only disagree.

An exegete, especially an Old Testament scholar, when studying the theme of this book, sees perhaps something that others do not discover so easily. It is to something of this sort that I would like to give expression. I hope that, despite renouncing any form of scholarly apparatus, something new will be made available for study and for the attention of colleagues. Others have contributed other things from their background to the by no means easy dialogue between Jews and Christians and must continue to do so. It is a gift of God that in the meantime there is such a dialogue. It can give us joy after so much endless pain.

Norbert Lohfink

Introduction

In recent years theological discussions about God's attitude to Judaism and Christianity have—besides the image of the way ("a twofold way to salvation")—often made use of the idea of "covenant." This word has acquired special importance, at least for Catholic partners in the dialogue, since Pope John Paul II spoke of the "old covenant" which has "never been revoked" in the presence of official Jewish representatives in Mainz in 1980.

Because of the significance that this papal statement has acquired in Jewish-Christian dialogue in recent years, the whole section of this much publicized statement is cited here:

> The first aspect of this dialogue, namely the meeting between the people of God of the old covenant, which has never been revoked by God (cf. Rom 11:29), and the people of God of the new covenant, is at the same time a dialogue within our church between the first and second part of its Bible.

The pope of course is speaking of the Jewish people of today. The biblical reference published with the text is to a passage in the New Testament: Rom 11:29. This is important because the formulation reflects a Christian point of view. The text speaks of *the* "old covenant." It continues shortly afterward with mention of the "people of today who belong to the covenant made with Moses." The text itself links the "old covenant" immediately with the "first part" of the Christian Bible.

By expressing himself in this way, Pope John Paul II is on the one hand entirely within the field of traditional Christian thought. He speaks of "the old covenant." On the other hand he makes a daring breakthrough inasmuch as he relates Rom 11:29 to this "old covenant." What is one to say exegetically to this usage? This is the subject of the present inquiry.

It encounters then something which in part has a quite different nuance. There is not the remotest intention of instructing the pope in any way. It is merely a matter of explaining from the Bible what is implied in a very brief formulation made in the course of his speech and almost, as it were, by the way. If at the end a somewhat different formulation may be preferred, then this is intended only as a continuation in biblical language of an encounter with the formulation itself. The formulation of the pope was the point of departure of this booklet and contributed to its title. But its place is within the broader context of the entire Jewish-Christian dialogue of our time.

It is no great surprise that, at least on the part of the Christian participants in this dialogue, there has been a search to put the communicative process under the heading "covenant." Talk of "covenant" does not play all that great a role in typical rabbinic Jewish tradition. But it does for Christians. Why?

Let us begin with the Bible. "Covenant" is an important category there for expressing Israel's relationship to God. The word is already entrenched in the Hebrew Bible in different ways. But more of this later. In the period of the second temple, even before the appearance of Jesus, "covenant" was almost a standard word among the Jewish people for the ancestral religion. The question as to where and when the "new covenant" announced by Jeremiah would come remained in the air. We know from the manuscripts from Qumran that the Essenes applied this promise to their own community and for their own time, not primarily for the end of the ages which they still waited for. The word "covenant" then was at the same time important and readily comprehensible in Jewish usage in that era.

The early Christian communities took up Jewish talk of the "new covenant" in the last supper tradition (Mt 26:28; Mk 14:24; Lk 22:20; 1 Cor 11:25). According to the Markan form of the tradition, Jesus said over the cup:

> This is my blood, the blood of the covenant, shed for many (Mk 14:24).

Matthew adds: "for the forgiveness of sins" (Mt 26:28). Paul and Luke witness to a somewhat different form of the last supper tradition. In Luke, the pronouncement over the cup runs:

> This cup, poured out for you, is the new covenant sealed in my blood (Lk 22:20).

The relative phrase, "poured out for you," is missing in Paul who is perhaps quoting an abbreviated form of the tradition (1 Cor 11:25).

The word "covenant" is common to all versions. The mention of the "new covenant" occurs in only one line of the tradition. It must remain open then whether Jesus himself used it. The version used in the liturgy of today speaks always of the "new covenant." Everyone who participates in the eucharist is well aware of the idea.

From the time of the early Christian communities on, talk of the "new covenant" claimed that the promise of Jeremiah of a "new covenant" had been fulfilled in Jesus and his atoning death. It is inconceivable that the claim could have been formulated in this way without there having been reference to the Jeremian oracle. The key notion in this was the eschatological forgiveness of sins. Jeremiah's text about the "new covenant" ends with the sentence:

For I will forgive their wrongdoing and remember their sin no more (Jer 31:34).

The allusion to this sentence is linked in the pronouncement over the cup in the last supper tradition with allusions to the blood of the animals with which Moses sprinkled the altar and the people on Sinai (Ex 24:6, 8), and to the ending of the fourth servant song of the book of Isaiah (Is 53:11–12).

Faced with this early Christian notion of a "new covenant" it was naturally but a short step to talk of "two covenants." And this is what Paul does in Gal 4:24. It is likely that on the basis of 2 Cor 3:14–15, where Paul speaks of the "old covenant" = "Moses," from which readings were taken ("Moses" being used for the books of Moses), Christians soon distinguished in the sacred writings included in their canon an "old" and a "new" testament, testament being a translation of the Greek *diathēkē*. This is further the standard translation in the Greek Bible of the Hebrew word *bĕrît* (= obligation, oath, covenant). No wonder that the word "covenant," as it also comes to designate the sacred writings, assumes a central place today in Christian consciousness.

In recent decades Christian-Jewish dialogue has at last begun. It was natural to arrive at different theological conceptions of the relationship to each other of the different ways to salvation in Judaism and Christianity when one ventured onto the truly theological level. And so, at least on the Christian side, the word "covenant" suggested itself to describe and classify the different theories.

In order therefore to explain the Jewish-Christian relationship, there have arisen "one covenant theories" in opposition to "two covenant theories," and recently even "many covenant theories." John T. Pawlikowski for example works with headings of this kind in his article "Judaism and Christianity" in the *Theologisches Realenzklopädie* (17, 1988, pp. 386–403). It is not necessary to describe these different theories in detail here.

In any case, the formulation of the pope at Mainz fits into this linguistic usage. The pope would scarcely have had any intention of deciding between these different theological approaches in his passing, but carefully considered, remark. He is, however, stressing something which in his opinion must be upheld: namely that even from the Christian point of view Judaism can apply the word "covenant" to itself, that God on his side has never revoked their "old covenant."

It does not seem all that important in this linguistic

game to decide what belongs specifically to the category of "covenant" (in contrast to other conceivable categories). Rather let the common conviction of Christian and Jew alike simply be taken for granted, namely that when God acts in the world as revealer and savior, he does not everywhere do so in the same way. Both sides are convinced that God sets a history in motion and by so doing makes use of a chosen group of people. He will establish his rule in the world as a whole by means of a "people" submissive to him. The word "covenant" is the common and general term for this relationship of God to a particular group through which he acts in the world.

The question therefore is not so much the precise meaning of the Hebrew and Greek words which we translate by "covenant," but how the history of revelation and salvation designated by it has run its course, and with which concrete group the "people" through which God pursues it is to be identified today. And so inasmuch as Christianity and Judaism both stake claims to be the place where the "covenant" is, everything reduces itself to the question as to how these two claims are to be judged and how they relate to each other.

In such dialogues there is not much point in tracing systematically and in detail the original meaning of the words for "covenant," the demonstrable development of their meaning within the Bible, or the precise nuances of the different covenant statements and covenant theologies in the biblical writings and in later Jewish and Christian traditions and theologies, however important and decisive that may be in itself. Old Testament scholars are engaged in an extensive, and at times very controversial, discussion on this matter. The dialogue however can very quickly focus its attention in essence on the statements about the "new covenant" because so much depends on them. The question must be put to these texts, and those that cohere with them, whether and in what sense they are dealing with different "covenants," and if so whether they cancel each other out or move side by side through the course of history.

I take in what follows the Christian text as my base of departure. I include from the very start the writings of the New Testament. What I say is within the realm of Christian theology. Jews are not obliged to take what is valid for me as valid for them. They can only note that one can arrive at such opinions by taking the Christian canon as a starting point. Naturally, it appears differently for Christian readers.

So that one may orient oneself quickly, I preface a thesis to each chapter. I make no claim for completeness in what I say. I am more concerned to look for clarifications of difficult or disputed passages and to express an opinion on current discussions. I am not conducting any polemics. Hence, I am not attempting to document, much less discuss, the literature in all its ramifications. Therefore I can forgo notes.

I

"New Covenant" and Christian Anti-Judaism

THESIS: The popular Christian concept of the "new covenant" encourages anti-Judaism.

When there is talk of the "old" and the "new" covenant the average Christian conceives things as if there are two covenants, one "old" and one "new." They followed each other. When Jesus the messiah came, the "old covenant" was replaced by the "new covenant."

This notion is encouraged further inasmuch as "testament" is often used instead of "covenant." Our normal, secular usage of speaking of an "old" and a "new" testament readily prevails. As a consequence of this an *old* testament becomes invalid when one goes to a notary and has a *new* testament drafted.

When we Christians speak of the "new covenant" we regard present day Jews as the descendants of those Jews who at one time did not find their way into the "new covenant." Because the "old covenant" no longer exists, they belong to *no* "covenant" anymore, even though, naturally, they think that they belong to the old, or rather the sole, "covenant." This is where the pope's formulation in Mainz fits in.

It is clear that such standard thinking continues to contribute to and nourish hidden anti-Judaism among Christians, and all this with the appearance of belonging to the very essence of Christian identity.

Does this not open an unbreachable gulf, create some sort of tragic situation? Is there not after all another possible attitude than that which presupposes an insuperable and subjective error in the partner to the dialogue, which must be met in the normal way with that moral tolerance demanded of the human person?

When each is convinced of the error of the other, genuine tolerance would indeed be a means whereby they could live at peace with each other and even in mutual respect and encouragement. One might say: Would that there had always been such tolerance. But such lofty virtue is sadly so rare.

A theological construction such as the end of the old and the arrival of the new "covenant" is too much for the average human intellect and the emotion that always wells up with every attempt to find a scapegoat; it precipitates actions and consequences which defame, even threaten contemporary Jews. Thence follows the shocking and shameful history of the relations of Christians to Jews which we know so well.

It is no surprise when the question is raised whether it would not be better to eliminate talk about the "new covenant" from the Christian vocabulary—or to dispose of it by speaking of two "covenants," one, the old and still alive, according to which contemporary Judaism lives, and one, the new, according to which Christians live, adding, as one must, that there is no reason for Jews to renounce theirs because the other, the Christian, is conceived of as being only for the "nations." Has not

Pope John Paul II almost come around to this point of view in his address in Mainz?

Questions like these have undoubtedly contributed to the development of theories of the "permanent covenant," of the two covenants and even of "several covenants." Behind all this lies the urgent problem of talk of the "new covenant" with its bitter consequences. I have formulated the first thesis so as to make this clear.

Be that as it may, we Christians cannot simply eliminate talk of the "new covenant." When one refers back to the Bible, and as a theologian one cannot avoid it, one encounters the word of necessity and in key contexts. One cannot regard these texts as unwritten or remove them from the canon. One must explain them clearly when they occur. It is only honest—and such every Christian is required to be—for Christians to see themselves as part of the "new covenant" as a preliminary to any explanation of what this means precisely. Otherwise they renounce Christian identity.

It is another question of course whether the Christian must always use this expression, given that in certain recent contexts it has perhaps become misleading or even dangerous. That is a first qualification. One can distinguish quite well between biblical language, the reality that it expresses, and current formulation.

But there is a further note to add. Unfortunately, most Christian theologians are not really clear about what the ideas of "covenant" and "new covenant" mean in their biblical origins and what function they have in the biblical writings. It is worthwhile then to look at it more closely. Perhaps one would not be so quick to replace it by other ideas when one understands it only as it is used in the Bible. Perhaps too one can then distin-

15

guish more readily, and by advancing reasons, between the very different "one-covenant," "two-covenant" and "multi-covenant" theories now available on the theological dialogue market.

If one does not look into the Bible more carefully than usual, one goes groping easily in other directions. Without having examined the texts with greatest care, one submits them to psychological and sociological explanations. Therefore, even before dealing with the texts themselves, I would like to state my position on a manner of treating talk of the "new covenant" in Jewish-Christian dialogue which is widespread today.

II

"New Covenant"—
A Contentious Idea
in the Early Church?

THESIS: When one says that the idea of the "new covenant" served from the very beginning to set Christians apart from Jews, and to marginalize Jews in the new Christian world view, one does not contribute to the explanation of the question of fact. Besides, this contention is by no means historically certain.

A common pattern of thinking is that the New Testament introduced the idea of the new covenant to set emerging Christianity apart from Judaism.

Realities, which by their very existence question one's own world view, must, according to the results of scientific sociology, be interpreted by a group in such a way that they become harmless either by negative trimming down or even by theoretical annihilation. Something of this sort has happened here. This is the contention today of theologians who are to be taken seriously. It is often said that the idea of the "new covenant" arose from the early Christian polemic of separation against

Judaism as it consolidated itself anew after the destruction of Jerusalem in the year 70.

There was such a separation of the newly emerging entity of Christianity from its native soil, Judaism. The writings of the New Testament also bear this stamp—and, given this context, probably talk of the "new covenant" as well. But this does not in any way explain everything.

First, it is logically illicit to do away with a problem area by saying that there were wrong motivations. The circumstances in which a thing is given spoken form, and the motives and emotions that the speaker thereby gives rise to, are important so as to understand the mood and the guiding perspectives. However the thing thus given spoken form can be independent of the situation and have a basis conditioned by lasting reality. But sociological and psychological considerations do not settle the question of truth.

Second, the question remains for me on the level of circumstances and motives whether talk of the "new covenant" is not older than the bitter dispute between Jewish and Christian brothers and sisters living their own separate lives. Even if the historical Jesus may not have introduced the "new covenant" as a key term at the last supper, was it not already part of anti-Jewish polemic and independent of it in the last supper tradition of the early Christian communities? Is it not further a typical example of *Jewish*-Christian language? The use of the phrase at Qumran shows that it was quite possible within Judaism at that time for a Jewish group to lay exclusive claim to talk of the "new covenant." This could indicate a separation from other Jewish groups, though not a removal from Judaism itself.

It is more likely, I think, that such was the occasion when the idea was introduced, and one can ask: Why? The expression "introduced," however, is quite ambiguous. The early Christians certainly did not create the idea. Its creator is the prophet Jeremiah or, if many scholars are correct, one of the "deuteronomistic" redactors of the book of Jeremiah in the generation after him. The basic text on the "new covenant" occurs in Jer 31:31–34. The early Christians merely took up the idea and applied it to themselves, as did the Qumran community.

And so, historically as well, things are not quite so simple. It is no help to allow oneself to be cowed all too quickly and meekly to the penitents' bench by the sociologists. The separation of Christians and Jews which happened so quickly certainly did not correspond to the will of God; it can only be described correctly by the category of sin. And even now, after almost two thousand years, this has not yet been cleansed. Nevertheless, in the concrete matter of the present inquiry into the phrase "new covenant," it must first be explained whether it was really associated with this event from the very beginning, and which were the motives that found expression in it in its later application to independent concrete questions.

III

An Auxiliary Notion—
And No More

THESIS: Rom 9:4; Acts 7:8; Eph 2:11–12; Lk 1:72–75; Acts 3:25–26; Gal 3:15–18; Gal 4:22–31; and Rev 11:19 can demonstrate that talk of the "covenant" even in the New Testament is not univocal and ought not to be taken too ontologically. It is a question of a theological auxiliary notion which is quite variable even in its constant allusion to this or that statement in the older biblical writings.

This chapter is something of a loosening up exercise before we turn our attention to texts about the "new covenant."

There are many "covenant theologies" in the field of the Old Testament. Each has its own constricted system of expressions which are not readily compatible. First, the earlier "deuteronomistic" talk in the Sinai or Horeb covenant is not immediately compatible with the "priestly" talk in the two interrelated "covenants" of God with Noah and Abraham, even when they occur in the one text of the Pentateuch and so, as it were, in one and the same context.

First, the word "covenant" has a very different meaning in each case. In the one case its meaning is something like a contract which can be broken and then is at an end (this is the original deuteronomistic notion); in the other, its meaning is rather a solemn promise made by God under oath which an unfaithful partner cannot simply destroy by his or her infidelity (this is the original priestly notion). The Hebrew word behind all this, berît, can make both statements. It is the context that determines which of the two possibilities is meant. Further, the priestly presentation of history, with the two great promises to the whole human race (in the post-diluvial ancestor, Noah) and to the chosen people (in the ancestor, Abraham), has deliberately suppressed from its historical plan the somewhat older notion of a contract-like covenant between God and the people of Israel on Mount Sinai.

Aside from these two basic "covenant theologies" there stand still other texts which speak at times in different ways of the "covenant." There are many passages where different statements of this kind have been combined in one final text fed from several sources. Once again they modify each other somewhat.

All this is of course only possible because we cannot speak of *the* "covenant" in the field of the Old Testament. There is "something" that is spoken about; there are images and ideas with which the biblical writers try to grasp what is meant by that "something"; and they can change. This is where talk about "covenant" belongs.

The "something" which is spoken about is God's relationship to particular persons, to his people, or to the whole human race. Just as one can use for this relationship the words "father" and "master," so too

21

one can use the word "covenant" and on each occasion with one nuance or another, with one reference or another. One of the various possibilities was, in looking to the future, to talk of a "new covenant." It belongs to the comprehensive area of tradition encompassed by the "deuteronomistic" covenant theology, though it gives this a prophetic turn toward the future. I have already emphasized in the introduction that at the time of Jesus, "covenant" had become a kind of general word which could designate simply the ancestral religion of the Jews, just as we speak of our (Christian) "faith." But this does not exclude that the word could be used, now in one sense, now in another, in the writings of early Christianity, even in the New Testament.

This was in fact the case. These eight passages show this: Rom 9:4; Acts 7:8; Eph 2:11-12; Lk 1:72-75; Acts 3:25-26; Gal 3:15-18; Gal 4:22-31; Rev 11:19.

At the beginning of chapter 9 of the letter to the Romans there is a detailed list of all the prerogatives of the Jews with respect to other peoples. In the middle of this list, after (God's) "sonship" (of Israel: already linked with the exodus) and the glory (of God dwelling among them), and before the law (bestowed on Sinai), the order of worship (likewise bestowed there), and the promises, stand in due order "the covenants," *hai diathēkai,* plural. The text runs:

> They are Israelites: they were made God's sons; theirs is the splendor of the divine presence; theirs the covenants, the law, the temple worship, and the promises. Theirs are the patriarchs, and from them in natural descent sprang the Messiah (Gk: the Christ) (Rom 9:4-5).

And so from the very outset, before there was any prospect of a "new covenant," the point of departure was that the entity "covenant" was already at hand in a variety of forms in the history of Israel; there were "covenants." This is in full accord with the biblical writings where Abraham was guaranteed a "covenant" and later several new covenants were struck: on Sinai, in the land of Moab, at Shechem, with David, with Levi, under Josiah of Jerusalem, and so on.

A point of view similar to that of Rom 9:4 occurs in the speech of Stephen in Acts 7. In the legal process in which he is the accused, he enumerates before the supreme council God's acts on behalf of his people Israel, in the middle of which, and in a very positive sense, there occurs once more the term "covenant." Stephen does not use the word elsewhere in the enumeration, though he might well have done so. The centerpiece in the rather long passage about Abraham reads:

> He gave him the covenant of circumcision, and so, after Isaac was born, he circumcised him on the eighth day; and Isaac begot Jacob, and Jacob the twelve patriarchs (Acts 7:8).

The reference is to the patriarchal narratives of Genesis, in particular to Gen 17:9–14 and 21:4. When the word "covenant" is used here, it is not a question of promise, but of the institution of an obligatory sign of membership of the community of the promise.

Reference to "covenants" in the plural occurs again in the letter to the Ephesians:

> Remember then your former condition: you, Gentiles as you are by birth, you, "the uncircumcised"

so called by those who are called "circumcised" (but only with reference to an outward rite)—you were at that time separate from Christ, strangers to the community of Israel, outside God's covenants and what goes with them (the promise). Your world was a world without hope and without God (Eph 2:11–12).

Israelites of the New Testament period who did not follow Jesus are not envisaged here. Israel which received the promise, and stands in opposition to the "uncircumcised," changes over directly into "Christ," the church. Both are seen as a unity, and those addressed were excluded from this one reality before they came to faith. The "covenants of the promise" also belong to this one reality. The qualifying genitive makes it clear once again that the perspective is that of the priestly and prophetic chain of Old Testament covenant texts, that is, the promise to Abraham and the other patriarchs, the promise to David, the promise of a "new" and an "eternal" covenant.

The prophetic hymn of Zechariah in the Lukan infancy story uses the key word "covenant" to speak of the promises. It is not however in the plural but in the singular; it speaks of a unique "holy covenant" which God has now remembered inasmuch as the forerunner of the messiah has been born. By means of parallelism, this "holy covenant" is qualified further as the "oath" which God "swore to our father Abraham." The content of the oath is given: rest from oppression by enemies. The whole text runs:

So he promised . . .
that he would deal mercifully with our fathers,

calling to mind his solemn covenant.
Such was the oath which he swore to our father
    Abraham,
    to rescue us from enemy hands,
and grant us, free from fear, to worship him
    with a holy worship, with uprightness of heart,
in his presence, our whole life long (Lk 1:72–75).

The phrase "rest from oppression by enemies" (v. 71) shows clearly that Gen 22:16–17 is in mind, because it is only there in the Abraham narratives that God assures Abraham under oath of the victory of his descendants over "their enemies." The use of the word "covenant" makes it clear that at the same time the totality of the biblical promises to Abraham is meant, for it is used only elsewhere for promises.

When one looks more closely, one finds that the perspective is primarily that of the cultic existence of Israel. This of course is characteristic of the priestly theology. However it does not, strictly speaking, appear in the Abraham narratives. It reveals itself in fact first as a retrospect in the series of statements referring to the covenant with Abraham in God's address to Moses in Ex 6:2–8. This (and in the announcement of this divine word in Ex 2:24) is the first mention in the Bible that God "remembers" his "covenant" with Abraham:

I have called my covenant to mind. Say therefore to the Israelites, "I am the Lord. I will release you from your labors in Egypt. I will rescue you from slavery there . . . I will adopt you as my people, and I will become your God" (Ex 6:5–7).

25

The text is opened up fully at the priestly climax of the institution of the sanctuary on Sinai:

> I shall dwell in the midst of the Israelites. I shall become their God (Ex 29:45).

These statements in the priestly writing in the book of Exodus, the last included, with its verb in the future, look back on the period of the institution of Israel. There is no echo at all of any promise that looks to a messianic future. However in the blessings of the holiness code, and as a result of the experience of the collapse of God's hitherto prevailing cult dispositions, the statements have been transformed into promises looking toward the future. In a distant future, when Israel has long been dispersed among the nations,

> I will remember my covenant with Jacob and my covenant with Isaac, yes, and my covenant with Abraham. . . . I will remember on their behalf the covenant with the men of former times whom I brought out of Egypt in full sight of all nations, that I might be their God. I am the Lord (Lev 26:42, 45).

There are echoes of all this, as well as of certain psalms (105:8; 106:45; 111:5), in these phrases of the "Benedictus." "Holy covenant" would further have special reference to the context of Lev 26 where the word "holy" is a sort of leitmotif.

The whole is concerned with the promise to the patriarchs which had been fulfilled long ago with Israel's induction into its land. Later, however, it was understood as a much broader promise. Several statements from the writings were attracted into the promise on oath to Abraham in the text from Lev 26 just cited as well as in the Sinai covenant.

Several promise texts from the patriarchal narratives of Genesis mingle together when Peter addresses his Jewish audience as "sons of the prophets and the covenant" (Acts 3) after the healing of the lame man in the temple. The covenant is defined thus:

> You are within the covenant which God made with your fathers, when he said to Abraham, "And in your offspring all the families of the earth shall find blessing." When God raised up his servant, he sent him to you first, to bring you blessing by turning every one of you from your wicked ways (Acts 3:25–26).

The passage cited appears, with slight variations, three times in the Abraham narratives of Genesis—12:3; 18:18; 22:18. The variations consist in this—that the blessing radiates from Abraham twice and from his descendants ("seed") once (22:18; originally meaning the same, of course), and, further, that once (12:3) all the "clans of the earth" and twice all the "nations of the earth" receive this blessing. However, the combination of the "seed" transmitting the blessing of Abraham to all "clans" does not occur. The three texts from the patriarchal narratives are to be read as a unity and combined with each other.

Moreover, the word "covenant" does not appear in these three passages. It comes up again in other formulations of the promises in the Abraham narratives where the key word "seed" is found. I will go into this below when dealing with the letter to the Galatians.

These passages too are to a certain extent drawn into the citation. It synthesizes the whole promise to the ancestral fathers, and does so under the key word "covenant."

For the rest, it synthesizes the texts in such a way that they speak right into the situation of decision into which Peter's audience are now placed in the temple area. *The* "seed" of Abraham is interpreted at once as the "servant" of God raised from the dead. It is Jesus. He communicates the promised blessing in this moment of fulfillment which has now arrived. And because he communicates it to all, Jews and pagans, and all must repent, the word "clans" and not "nations" is used for the recipients in the formulation of the promise. Thus, the Jews who were addressed could feel themselves included more easily than under the word "nations" which would have made them think only of others and not of themselves.

This understanding of the word "seed" is found also in Paul. It is proposed quite explicitly there. And so I come to the passages in the letter to the Galatians.

In Gal 3:6–19 the difference between what is feasible under the "law" and the range of the "promise" is expounded. The details of the thought process, in part very difficult, need not be discussed here. In any case, according to Paul, there was a basic promise made to Abraham long before the law was given on Sinai. This promise, which Paul thinks of as something of a proto-evangelium, 3:8, is fulfilled in Christ and in all who have received the promised Spirit from him.

To demonstrate that the promise spans the law, Paul introduces the word *diathēkē* into the middle of his discourse; it is the word for "covenant" in the Greek Bible which in the context can only be translated by its normal Greek meaning of "testament" (3:15).

The promises addressed to Abraham are, according to Paul, like a "testament" which can neither be rendered simply invalid nor altered by codicils. Hence, the law of Sinai regarding Abraham's descendants can abrogate nothing in God's "testament," i.e., in the promise of blessing for all nations made to Abraham (3:17). The crucial text runs:

> My brothers, let me give you an illustration: even in ordinary life, when a man's will and testament have been duly executed, no one else can set it aside or add a codicil. Now the promises were pronounced to Abraham and to his "issue." It does not say "issues" in the plural, but in the singular, "and to your issue"; and the "issue" intended is Christ. What I am saying is this: a testament, or covenant, had already been validated by God; it cannot be invalidated, and its promises rendered ineffective, by a law made four hundred and thirty years later (Gal 3:15–17).

One might think perhaps that the word *diathēkē*, the same word as elsewhere when there is talk of the "covenant," was used here more by chance, and that Paul did not have any intention at all of alluding to one of the statements about covenant in the Old Testament. But that is unlikely.

Like Peter in Acts 3:25–26, Paul here and in the neighboring text draws together the different promise texts from the Abraham narratives of Genesis into one single promise. He takes the content of the promise

29

from Gen 12:3; 18:18; 22:18, which is his concern in the context of his argumentation, namely blessing for the nations. He is concerned precisely with the nations in contrast to Israel. He takes the singular expression "your seed" from Gen 12:7; 13:15; 15:18; 17:7; 22:18; 24:7, which allows him to conclude to Christ as the one whom the promise is really addressing. Three of these last named passages describe the promise as sworn on solemn oath: 15:18; 17:7; 24:7. The word used is *berît* in Gen 15:18; 17:7, rendered in Greek by *diathēkē* and translated usually in our versions of the Bible by "covenant."

Gen 15 and 17 are the two Genesis texts about the covenant with Abraham. The word *berît* must be understood in these two chapters as a direct promise by God under oath. It is only a short step thence to the notion of a "testament," and in Greek not so much as even that.

Paul is taking over completely here on Old Testament covenant theology. It is a different one to that which was to the fore when talking of the "new covenant." The latter refers back to the Sinai covenant and develops from it the assurance of another, future "covenant." Here, in chapter 3 of the letter to the Galatians, everything belonging to Sinai proceeds under the key word "law," and the *diathēkē* opposed to it, the only one in this word-play, is on the one hand older than the law and on the other overarches it up to the present moment of its fulfillment. According to the thought pattern of this text Christians belong not to a "new covenant" but to the "Abraham covenant" which both precedes and overarches the law of Sinai.

The next chapter shows at once how free is the speech here. Once again it is a matter of a text which in its details and thought process is very difficult, at least for us today. And once again it is not necessary to give an exegesis of the whole text.

Gal 4:22–31 is concerned further with the opposition between those, both Jew and pagan, who have come to faith in Christ following the promise to Abraham, and those whose identity is determined by the law of Sinai. The text puts Abraham's son Isaac, the son of Sarah the free woman, in one group and Abraham's son Ishmael, the son of Hagar the maidservant, in the other. One group is the earthly Jerusalem, the other the heavenly. Third, he speaks of the "two covenants." The main lines of thought are as follows:

> It is written there that Abraham had two sons, one by his slave and the other by his free-born wife. The slave-woman's son was born in the course of nature, the free-woman's through God's promise. This is an allegory. The two women stand for two covenants. The one bearing children into slavery is the covenant that comes from Mount Sinai; that is Hagar. Sinai is a mountain in Arabia, and it represents the Jerusalem of today, for she and her children are in slavery. But the heavenly Jerusalem is the free woman; she is our mother. . . . And you, my brothers, like Isaac, are children of God's promise (Gal 4:22–26, 28).

Paul in fact draws out the theme of the two covenants, as one can see, only for the line of "Hagar—earthly Jerusalem—those under the law." The question arises, then, to what extent he can describe the other line "Sarah—heavenly Jerusalem—those of the promise through faith" as a "covenant." For he speaks to be sure of "two covenants."

31

It is often thought that the background here is simply the primitive Christian tradition of the last supper with its conviction of the "new covenant" in the blood of Christ. There is no denying that this is involved. However, there are other associations in the text which more readily suggest themselves.

First, there could be further echoes of the allusion to the Abraham covenant of chapter 3. For the link with chapter 3 is otherwise quite strong. It continues dealing with the true descendants of Abraham, as was the case there, and in the two key passages the theme word from there occurs again: "promise" (4:23, 28). The thought then is still colored by the original opposition between the deuteronomistic notion of covenant ("Sinai covenant": "covenant" as contract and law) and the priestly notion ("Abraham covenant": "covenant" as promise and oath). Whereas in chapter 3 the word "covenant" is employed only for the one side of the opposition, namely the promise to Abraham, here it is employed for both sides, the promise as well as the Sinai covenant, whereby the difference is made quite clear. It is possible to derive both from the older biblical texts, and thus it can be seen how freely the word "covenant" can be used.

But things are even more complicated. Paul characterizes one of the opposed entities as the heavenly Jerusalem by a citation from Is 54:1 in a verse that was omitted above:

> Rejoice, O barren woman who never bore a child;
> break into a shout of joy, you who never knew a
>   mother's pangs;
> for the deserted wife shall have more children
> than she who lives with the husband (Gal 4:27).

32

The passage in Isaiah which this verse introduces moves finally to its conclusion:

> These days recall for me the days of Noah:
> as I swore that the waters of Noah's flood
> should never again pour over the earth,
> so now I swear to you
> never again to be angry with you or reproach you.
> Though the mountains move and the hills shake,
> my love shall be immovable and never fail,
> and my covenant of peace shall never be shaken.
> So says the Lord who takes pity on you.

Did Paul want to call to mind this "covenant" which occurs at the end of the passage which he intoned? And if so, did he regard it as a divine promise at the time of the prophet Isaiah or did he equate it with the "new covenant" of the last supper tradition?

Who knows? It is but a question of associations echoing in the background. Everything may well have been left open deliberately. If the covenant with Noah appears in the Isaian text as an object of comparison, then a bridge is thereby thrown across to the corresponding Abraham covenant in Genesis. In any case, it is clear once more with what a variety of nuances the word "covenant" can be used in the New Testament.

It appears as a standard symbol at one of the high points in the book of Revelation of John after the Lamb has opened the seventh seal of the heavenly book and the seven angels have blown the seven trumpets. The seventh trumpet proclaims that God now inaugurates definitively his sovereignty. At this moment the heavenly temple of God opens and reveals within it the ark of the covenant. At the same time there is lightning, thunder, an earthquake and hail (Rev 11:19). This alludes to the description of the theophany in Ex 19. The "ark of the covenant" derives its name from the Sinai context, and the "covenant" here is none other than the decalogue which, written on tablets of stone, is kept in this ark (cf. Deut 5).

This is an entirely different use of the word "covenant" from that in the passages dealt with so far. What this visionary image intends to say is not to be explained immediately. Is it saying something about the continuity between the beginning of God's sovereignty in Israel and its consummation? Is it speaking of the transcendence or its opposite? Standard symbols are often open to several explanations. In any case, the word "covenant" is simply playing once more on certain places in the scriptures with, however, different nuances of meaning.

So then, by way of synthesis: As in the Hebrew Bible, so too in the New Testament writings, "covenant" is something very different from a formula which describes definitively something which is quite fixed. It is rather an idea which, depending on its application, refers now to this, now to that thing. What this thing is should be derived on each occasion from the context. Further, there is a constant play on particular Old Testament passages without an understanding of which the New Testament passages cannot really be understood correctly.

When one talks therefore of the "new covenant" it is less important that it seems to be expressing something opposed to the "old covenant" than that it is referring to a prophetic oracle of promise in the book of Jeremiah. What more is to be said about the idea "old covenant"?

IV

The "Old Covenant" According to 2 Cor 3:14

THESIS: The idea "old covenant" does not occur at all in the Hebrew Bible. It occurs once only in the New Testament in 2 Cor 3:14. No opposition between the two "covenants" is set up there, nor is there an end to the "old" when the "new" comes. The thought pattern is that of unveiling and excelling. In a certain sense there is but a single covenant.

A careful reading of the text about the "new covenant" in Jer 31 leads to a surprising result: a "new covenant" is promised, but the words "old covenant" are not there. They are nowhere to be found in the whole of the "Old Testament," although now Christians describe that part of the sacred scriptures thus. Even in the "New Testament" they occur only once, in 2 Cor 3:14, although other texts, the letter to the Hebrews for example, come very close to the notion of the "old covenant."

This does not mean that such terminology ("old covenant"—"new covenant") could not have been in use in the Christian communities before Paul. The ready manner in which Paul handles the ideas in 2 Cor 3 suggests this. However, that the letter to the Hebrews, where one would most expect it, does not develop the idea of the "old covenant" speaks against it. But were there such pre-Pauline terminology, then the two ideas will have grown up in the context of the last supper tradition. Nevertheless, in our scripture the expression "old covenant" is found only in 2 Cor 3.

But we must ask: What sort of echo does this passage have in the context in which it stands? Is not Paul working out a sharp contrast between "old" and "new covenant," as was Jeremiah, even though the word is missing?

Earlier, that seemed obvious to me. In the meantime however I have doubts based on a more accurate analysis of the text—and that, even though 2 Corinthians is "polemical" throughout. It is worthwhile examining the text more closely.

First, it might be noted that in 2 Corinthians Paul does not intend to give anything like a commentary on the Jeremiah passage. This prophetic word is nowhere quoted in the genuine Pauline texts. Paul does not seem to cite the book of Jeremiah at all in the strict sense. This does not mean that he did not know it or that he could not allude to it. However it does not seem that he possessed a Jeremiah scroll and carried it with him on his travels. Because he obviously and always tested his literal citations of biblical passages against the biblical text, he avoided literal citations from the book of Jeremiah, as also from the book of Ezekiel, of which he likewise had no scroll.

In any case, he is commenting in 2 Cor 3 on a passage from the Sinai narratives in the book of Exodus about Moses' veiled countenance (Ex 34:29–35). At least he goes stealthily through this text and draws many a literal formula from it. It all begins quite early in 2 Cor 3:7 where he speaks of the letters chiseled in stone. He is referring of course to the tables of the decalogue in Ex 34:29.

Nevertheless, it would be foolish to say that because of this Paul could not at the same time remind his readers of Jeremiah's prophecy when he introduces the idea of the "new covenant" and expands it with that of the "old covenant." Moreover, there are too many other motifs in 2 Cor 3 from the Jeremiah passage on the "new covenant" and from its parallels in Jeremiah and Ezekiel for one to see reference exclusively to the last supper tradition whenever there is talk of the "new covenant."

When one reads the text of 2 Cor 3, one must be careful to note that its real theme is apostolic service. The comparison of the two covenants is subordinate to this and serves only to illustrate the dimension of the mandate of the Christian mission:

> The qualification we have comes from God. It is he who has qualified us to dispense his new covenant—a covenant expressed not in a written document, but in a spiritual bond; for the written law condemns to death, but the Spirit gives life.
>
> The law, then, engraved letter by letter upon stone, dispensed death, and yet it was inaugurated with divine splendor. That splendor, though it was soon to fade, made the face of Moses so bright that the Israelites could not gaze steadily at him. But if so, must not even greater splendor rest upon the divine dispensation of the Spirit? If splendor accompanied the dispensation under which we are condemned, how much richer in splendor must that one be under which we are acquitted! Indeed,

37

the splendor that once was is now no splendor at all; it is outshone by a greater splendor still. For if that which was soon to fade had its moment of splendor, how much greater is the splendor of that which endures!

With such a hope as this we speak out boldly; it is not for us to do as Moses did; he put a veil over his face to keep the Israelites from gazing on that fading splendor until it was gone. But in any case, their minds had been made insensitive, for that same veil is there to this very day when the lesson is read from the old covenant, it not being revealed that it is at an end in Christ. [Translator's note: "but . . . Christ": very different from the NEB which reads: "and it is never lifted, because only in Christ is the old covenant abrogated"; "it," the subject of "is at an end," is the "veil," *not* the "old covenant."] But to this very day, every time the law of Moses is read, a veil lies over the minds of the hearers. However, as scripture says, "whenever one turns to the Lord the veil is removed." Now the Lord of whom this passage speaks is the Spirit, and where the Spirit of the Lord is, there is liberty. And because for us there is no veil over the face, we all reflect as in a mirror the splendor of the Lord; thus we are transfigured into his likeness, from splendor to splendor; such is the influence of God who is Spirit (2 Cor 3:5b–18).

This text is permeated with hyperbolic thinking. The "new covenant" surpasses the "old" in splendor. However, the text is not easy to translate where the statement which is important for us occurs. In order to understand it properly, one must take as one's point of departure that in the synagogues the torah scrolls (and so the writings which report the covenant on Sinai) were veiled with a fine piece of cloth. Paul is alluding to this liturgical practice. He says: there is a veil over the "old covenant" right up to this very day. And for the end of the verse I support Luther's translation: this veil is a cover "which discontinues in Christ." [Translator's note: the author notes here that the *Einheitsübersetzung* is incorrect; namely, that because of this covering there remains veiled that "it," i.e. "the old covenant" which "comes to an end in Christ." NEB reads essentially the same: "and it [the veil] is never lifted, because only in Christ is the old covenant abrogated."]

It is not then the "old covenant" but the veil over the "old covenant" that comes to an end, just as in the Exodus narrative the veil on the shining and hence normally veiled countenance of Moses was always removed when he entered the sanctuary. According to Paul, something similar happens in the "new covenant" to all who believe in Christ. What is true of Moses is true also of them. God's "splendor" is reflected in them. They have all entered the sanctuary. No veil must cover the "splendor" any longer for them.

What was covered over previously was the "old covenant." It was the shining object to which one could not expose oneself. Now one can expose oneself to it as Moses did because all have entered the sanctuary. So the "old covenant," unveiled, gleams in the "new covenant" in God's splendor which shines from it. It is in no wise abolished or at an end, nor could it be forgotten. The "new covenant" is nothing else than the unveiled, no longer covered "old covenant" which radiates God's splendor already contained in it.

We can speak of Paul's statement about the unveiling as belonging to the topos of hyperbole, not to the topos of the end or the process of terminating the "old covenant." This could not perish because Paul presupposes that "now," where the ministers of the "new covenant" are ever on their way in the world, the lesson is still read from it.

We have, I think, difficulties with this interpretation, especially because we associate other reactions with the word pair "old—new" than did the people of old. For us moderns, who are conditioned by the process of evolution and constant process, what is newer is always something other. The old must yield to the new. For the people of old, the word pair could also have such echoes. But that is not necessarily the case. One gave for the most part the ancients the credit of greater originality and resilience. What was new was the exhausted, the degenerate, decadent. The word "new" took on positive associations only when one could say: the new brings the ancient to light anew.

V

The Letter to the Hebrews: Shadow and Reality

THESIS: The letter to the Hebrews does not use the term "old covenant." But it sets up a real opposition between the two "covenants." The "first" is doomed to disappear when the "second" comes. Yet what it says might well be transposed into the hyperbolic thinking of 2 Corinthians.

Here I would like to state the weightiest objection that could be constructed against the interpretation proposed of 2 Cor 3:14. The letter to the Hebrews as a matter of fact also speaks of the "old covenant," although it does not use the expression directly. And is not "old" used there in the sense of "outmoded" or "outdated"?

Let us cite the main passage in Heb 8:13. After using literally the promise of a "new covenant" from the book of Jeremiah, the author of the letter continues:

> By speaking of a new covenant, he (God or Jeremiah) has pronounced the first one grown old; and anything that is growing old and aging will shortly disappear.

Is not the idea of the "old covenant" to be deduced in a certain fashion from this passage in the book of Jeremiah, and with entirely negative echoes? And further, is it not said that Jesus is the "mediator of a better covenant" (8:6), and that "that first covenant" was not "faultless" and so a "second" must take its place (8:7)? Several chapters continue this theme further, and in 10:1 it is said that the law (of Moses) "contains but a shadow, and no true image, of the good things which were to come"— in obvious contrast to the "new covenant" that has come with Christ.

There is clearly talk here of two "covenants," whereby the "first" is inferior to the "second" and rendered obsolete by it.

This text must be taken in all seriousness. This and like passages are certainly the source of that basic Christian feeling which has persisted in talk about the "old covenant" and has had those bitter consequences in the course of history with which we are all familiar.

But let a warning be sounded at once! It would not be correct to reinterpret the text of 2 Cor 3 from the letter to the Hebrews be it ever so often and forever so long that it may have been read in the light of Hebrews. In the former, the "old covenant" is not at an end but only begins to shed its full light in the "new."

That means of course that we have to reckon with a contradiction within the New Testament. But is it more than a contradiction of different ways of thinking? And why should there not be different ways of thinking side by side in the biblical canon whose opposition can only be resolved when one stands back from the formulations?

If that is conceded, then the question can arise:

Which way of thinking should be preferred in the theology and proclamation of today? That is of course a most important question. It can only be answered properly if one delves deeply into the categories and realm of thought which stamps the letter to the Hebrews. I cannot go into a long and necessarily detailed discussion of the categories which Hebrews uses to make its statements. I will try to indicate briefly what is of importance. On the one hand, the letter to the Hebrews goes back to the Old Testament more often and more systematically than the other New Testament writings—perhaps less to the world of contemporary Judaism, because the temple cult in Jerusalem would be functioning no longer when the letter was composed. On the other hand, it does so in a way that is very Greek, or, more accurately, very Alexandrine, in manner. The contrast of "shadow" and "reality" of the "good things to come" in the passage just cited makes this clear. It is the language of "inculturation."

Inasmuch as we find it much more difficult to handle points of view which derive ultimately from Plato than those which conform immediately to the Old Testament ways of thinking, we nowadays approach the matter under discussion much rather from the 2 Cor letter—and this all the more so when our partners in the dialogue are Jews. And so when we are today looking for the correct theological language, we should take our lead rather from the second letter to the Corinthians than from the letter to the Hebrews.

As regards the letter to the Hebrews itself, it should be pointed out further that despite the twofold "covenant" of which it speaks and despite the negative evaluation of the idea "old," it does not refer to the "first covenant" merely in negative terms. The relationship between the two "covenants" is based on the idea of "image" and "reality," and this means not only opposition, but foremost positive correspondence.

For this reason I think that attempts to translate the letter to the Hebrews into the language of 2 Cor are by no means hopeless. One can also express what the letter intends to say by speaking of one covenant only which now becomes "new" when it is freed from a veil and begins to shine in an entirely different way.

Jer 31: A Single "Covenant"

THESIS: Jer 31:31–34 as well is not really speaking of two "covenants" but only of one. Israel has broken it. God will institute it anew. The unity of the covenant is established through its same content. It is characterized not only by torah and the covenant formula, but also by the gift of the land and the blessed life as a people in the land bestowed.

Jer 31:31–34, the text which is the background to the statements in the New Testament about the "new covenant," does not contain, as already noted, the words "old covenant."

But the question naturally arises: Does it not establish an opposition between the "covenant" which God made with Israel at the exodus from Egypt and the "new covenant" promised for the future? Is not the text more in line with the letter to the Hebrews than with 2 Corinthians?

Immediately on reading the text, one senses how rhetorical is its style and how it derives its form entirely from contrasts. The translation follows the Hebrew text. Later, when discussing Rom 9–11, we will have to go back to the old Greek text as well. It runs:

The time is coming, says the Lord, when I will make a new covenant with Israel and Judah. It will not be like the covenant I made with their fore-fathers when I took them by the hand and led them out of Egypt. This covenant of mine they broke although I was their master, says the Lord (author's version of v. 32b). But this is the covenant which I will make with Israel after those days, says the Lord; I will set my law within them and write it on their hearts; I shall become their God and they shall become my people. No longer need they teach one another to know the Lord; all of them, high and low alike, shall know me, says the Lord, for I will for-give their wrongdoing and remember their sin no more.

However, the obviously rhetorical character of the language once again awakens some doubts. What is really opposed to what? In this whirlpool of opposites, what is just language but perhaps does not touch the reality? Past and present are certainly set in opposition to each other. The past is determined by Israel's breach of the "covenant," the future by God's forgiveness and the institution of a "new covenant." If one asks whether this is a "covenant" other than the first, broken one, then one learns with amazement at least one thing: this "new covenant" too is concerned with God's torah. It is not said that God will give a new torah. It is therefore the same torah.

One must understand the text intelligently. With regard to the "covenant" from the time of the exodus, it is not stated explicitly that it also centered around God's torah. Nor is it stated explicitly that the breach of the "covenant" was naturally the non-observance of the torah, because in the world of the book of Jeremiah and the realm of the deuteronomistic language out of which the entire text comes, this is simply taken for granted. The same holds for the statement: "I will become their God and they shall become my people." This was also the summary formula for the covenant from the period of Israel's youth. This, known as the "covenant formula," is expanded in the crucial passage of the deuteronomic law, Deut 26:17–19. The deuteronomic law is that concrete form of the torah that the book of Jeremiah has in mind.

This very content at least is common alike to the broken "covenant" and the promised "new covenant": God institutes between himself and Israel that special God-people relationship which is expressed in the "covenant formula," and Israel takes over the torah. From the standpoint of this actual content, it is clearly a question of the same "covenant."

However, the text is not thereby fully exhausted. Things are said about the "new covenant" of the future which clearly do not hold for the earlier. It is not a question of the basic structure and content of the "covenant" but, so to formulate it, of its fragility. The earlier "covenant" was in fact broken. Hence, it must have been given to Israel in such a way that it could be broken. The "new covenant" will be given in a new way; it will be something within, with a torah written on the heart, it not being necessary to teach it from without. If one takes the rhetorical antitheses seriously, that means: because the "new covenant" is founded within the person, within, so to speak, the realm of freedom itself, it can no more undergo the fate of the earlier "covenant" and so be broken. This touches on the mystery of the cooperation between God and human freedom in regard to the "new covenant." It is at the very summit of this cooperation at which the human person in complete freedom is taken up entirely into the will of God.

I would rather not in this place pursue further what is hinted at here, important though it may be to do so, and however rarely, unfortunately, it is done when talking of the "new covenant." I will return to it later. Can one not suggest that here too, as with Paul, a similar thought pattern lies before us: that the new covenant is but the earlier one, now brilliant and radiant?

That's just what I think. Despite all the rhetorical counterpoint, what lies hidden in the Jeremiah text is not the rationale of the completely different, utterly outmoded earlier one, the purer antithesis, but the fuller and more lasting actualization of what was given of old.

The "covenant" in question is that which God had made with Israel when he "took them by the hand and led them out of Egypt" (31:32). It is that which we call the "Sinai covenant." This covenant was not "outmoded" but "broken" (31:32). It became then nonexistent. If it were to come to life again, it must be guaranteed anew by God. Only in this way could there be a "new" covenant. Hence too the word "new."

This certainly means more than that Israel is renewing itself interiorly in the spirit of torah loyalty after this loyalty had faded notably in the meantime—more than a ritual of covenant renewal, something like the renewal of vows that takes place regularly in many religious communities. It means in fact that God pardons and institutes again and anew the old that has been lost. But it is the old. It is not another "covenant."

48

Nevertheless, we must be much more concrete in exegeting this text. At the time that it was composed there was a sign visible to all of the broken covenant—the destruction of Jerusalem in the year 587 B.C.E. and the deportation to Babylon. These events constitute the situation which is the point of departure of chapters 30 and 31 of the book of Jeremiah. There must also have been a sign visible to all of the renewal of the covenant by the God of Israel. When we think along the lines of precise correspondence, it must be the return of the exiles and the beginning of a new life in Jerusalem. The text speaks just of this as well, though it is rarely noted.

Return and pardon are the two statements which, belonging together, frame the whole Jeremian text of the "new covenant." This is vastly more comprehensive than the few verses of Jeremiah usually quoted, 31:31–34. The unity that deals with the "new covenant" begins with the first verses of chapter 30, and its first theme is the promise of the return from exile.

The theological literature virtually never mentions that the "new covenant" in Jeremiah has anything to do with the return from the Babylonian exile. It is amazing how it recedes into the background in Old Testament exegetical literature. This accords with the practice of systematic theology which often uses the biblical text as a quarry for brief, passing citations, and of exegesis which allows itself to fall too heavily under a literary-critical or form-critical statement of the question. In both cases too little attention is paid to the textual context. It is especially necessary to do so in this concrete case while making use of appropriate form and literary critical study.

Let us try then to search out these contexts in the text itself of Jer 30–31. The only text from Jeremiah that is usually cited, 31:31–34, begins:

> The time is coming, says the Lord, when . . . (Jer 31:31).

This introductory sentence with its definite style can lead us to the text as a whole. The same formula is already there in Jer 30:3:

> . . . this is the very word of the Lord: The time is coming when I will restore the fortunes of my people Israel and Judah, says the Lord, and bring them back to the land which I gave to their forefathers; and it shall be their possession.

(Translator's note: the author points out a misunderstanding in the *Einheitsübersetzung* of the last two lines; this error does not appear in the NEB. What must be made clear, the author notes, is that "return to the land of Israel in the days to come is promised to the exiles.")

There follows after 30:3 in the book of Jeremiah a long poetic insertion. It is an important text from the prophet's early period which in a certain sense furnishes the basis of the promise of return and covenant renewal which provides the frame. In the later stages of the redaction of the book it has been expanded by other oracles. It is only in 31:27 that the wording of the beginning occurs again, and it continues from the point where the other texts had been inserted, linking with 30:3:

> The time is coming, says the Lord, when I will sow Israel and Judah with the seed of man and the seed of cattle.

Not only return and new possession of the land are promised, but also, and very concretely, new increase of people and new earthly blessing. And a third and final "the time is coming" links up with this text, namely our text on the "new covenant." It extends the promise to its ultimate breadth. It brings the whole to a close with the basic passage already cited above:

> for I will forgive their wrongdoing and remember their sins no more (Jer 31:34).

This basis holds good for the *whole* text, 30:3–31:34; it is stated only once, although it presupposes all that has been proclaimed. Return, new possession of the land, increase in numbers, new prosperity, new covenant—all will come into effect together in the "days that are coming" because the God of Israel is disposed to forgive his people. All this, utterly concrete and utterly material, is first and foremost the "Jeremian" promise of the "new covenant."

It is thus in direct continuity with what constituted the "covenant" which God made with his people when he took it by the hand and led it out of Egypt. What God instituted then covered not only the law itself. It included the gift of the land, the making of a people, and material blessing, and then the torah for life in the land: a social order filled with prosperity.

As soon as one perceives this, quite new questions arise which are scarcely put by Christian theologians. Historically, the exiles did return after some decades.

VII

When Did God Fulfill the Promise of Jer 31?

THESIS: The fulfillment of the Jeremian promise of a "new covenant" cannot be fixed at a precise point in history. The promise was fulfilled with the return from exile and the rise of the new temple community around Jerusalem. Ps 51:12 shows that the new heart, loyal to the torah, as a new creation of God, was, at that time, available on request to the sinner who repented. Nevertheless, at the same time everything remained open for an eschatological-christological fulfillment.

If we ask: Has God forgiven his people again and once more taken up the "covenant" after the exile situation, presupposed by Jeremiah, had set in? Then it would simply be flouting the Bible as well as the historical facts to say that, since that event, God has not forgiven his people anymore nor has he had any dealings with them in history.

Israel has in fact returned from exile, something by no means common in human history. The new beginning in Jerusalem was the concrete form of God's pardon. The history of Israel with God went further even though a number of other catastrophes were involved in it, and though later a prophet like John the Baptist took as the starting point of his preaching that Israel had fallen fully under judgment again, and Paul at the beginning of the letter to the Romans includes Jews and pagans together under sin. The "covenant" was renewed. And that means: the "new covenant" that was announced had come.

Must one then conclude on the contrary that the text on the "new covenant" can have nothing to do with Jesus of Nazareth and Christianity? That would not be right either.

It is beyond doubt that the prophecy of Jer 30–31 was very soon fulfilled in its primary sense in the return from exile. Only, like most prophetic oracles of this type, it takes on a perspective and envisages an eschatological sort of fulfillment. This depth dimension of many prophetic proclamations only found its way into consciousness in the centuries that followed. The credit for this belongs above all to emergent apocalyptic. The question remains then: Even if there was once more a "covenant" between God and his people, did the oracle of the "new covenant" achieve its fullness of depth in subsequent history, and when?

It is here that we arrive at that which is proclaimed as really new in the promised "new covenant." It is, as we have seen, the promise that God's torah will no longer be something that instructs from outside the person, but will be inscribed on the heart:

> I will set my law within them and write it on their hearts; I will become their God and they shall become my people. No longer need they teach one

another to know the Lord; all of them, high and low alike, shall know me (Jer 31:33–34).

Is that what really happened when the exiles returned home from Babylon? Was the torah written on their hearts, even though it be on the heart of one single person, in such a way that this heart was entirely one with the torah so that it had no need to be instructed anymore about it? Was there one human heart which so captivated God that it became impossible for him ever again to regard his covenant as broken? Has God ever come to the point of "portraying" one human heart in such a way?

We Christians believe: there was such a heart. We refer to Jesus of Nazareth, to the "heart of Jesus." And we are convinced that all who bind themselves to this heart in faith, even when they themselves fail continually and must obtain pardon again, share in the strength of its fidelity to the torah, in its deeply rooted knowledge of God. And it is in it that we see a fulfillment of the promise of the "new covenant" which surpasses all that preceded it, *the* fulfillment of itself.

We must ask Jews who do not see it this way to respect our belief even though they do not share it. But when they regard such a complete fulfillment of the "new covenant" as something still outstanding and pray for it as a future good, we may never deny to them the loving and ever forgiving affection of God and thereby the renewal of the once broken "covenant" of Sinai. The oracle of Jeremiah has already been fulfilled positively and in a true sense in their history. The fulfillment began long before Jesus came.

We should never do them the injustice of thinking

that the partial fulfillment in their favor was merely material and external, that it never touched their heart. That would be to deny the scope of the Jeremian oracle of the "new covenant" and would above all do scant justice to Ps 51, the "Miserere." Ps 51:12 shows that even before the post-exilic rebuilding of the walls of Jerusalem God disposed to confer on Israel the very essence of the promised "new covenant," a heart stamped with the torah. Let this be developed a little further.

The oracle of the "new covenant" is not an erratic piece in the Hebrew writings. If it does not appear under the key word "new covenant," the same promise occurs in fact and with many corresponding formulations in the books of Jeremiah and Ezekiel, and several times again in Deut 30; in each new version it has been pondered over more profoundly. The torah can really be written on the human heart only when it is itself no longer something old. The human person must acquire a "new heart" so that the "new covenant" becomes a reality. The most important passages where the oracle of the "new covenant" is deepened are: Deut 30:1–14; Jer 24:5–7; 32:36–41; Ez 11:17–20; 16:59–63; 36:24–28. The key word "heart" occurs in Deut 30:6, 14; Jer 24:7; 32:39–40; Ez 11:19; 36:26. In Ez 36:26–27 it is linked with mention of a "new spirit." The word "covenant," not as "new" but as "eternal" (= irrevocable), appears in Jer 32:40; Ez 16:60; 37:26. We are dealing here with the same prophetic promise of salvation in ever fresh variations from the period of the exile and the dispersion of Israel. Talk of the "new covenant" was only one of the possible formulations. One of the most prominent elements is the talk of the new heart, a heart of flesh, a heart that in the long run is deeply disposed to repentance, the fear of God, the observance of God's will.

Talk which is strikingly similar, namely of a "clean heart" and of a "ready spirit," which God is to create in the sinner who prays for forgiveness, resounds at the high point of the well-known penitential psalm, the "Miserere":

> Create a pure heart in me, O God,
> and give me a new and steadfast spirit (Ps 51:12[10]).

There are other passages in this psalm which are close to the prophetic texts of the exile. The psalm in its present form comes from a period when perhaps many had already returned from exile. Return was at least possible. But the walls of Jerusalem had not yet been rebuilt. Prayer for the rebuilding occurs at the end of the psalm (51:20[18]). In any case, this is the period to which the psalm as a whole is to be assigned, whether the concluding prayer was originally part of it, or only added later.

One may contest whether an older version of the "Miserere," and perhaps also other similar prayers no longer preserved, served as models for the formulation of the prophetic promises, or whether on the contrary this psalm is the later text and depends on the prophetic promise already available and known in Israel. At least at the moment when the psalm and the prophetic promises were there together in the one canon of biblical writings—and that was certainly so before the time of Jesus—one could only pray the psalm in the light of the prophetic promises which were so closely related to it.

This means that already before Christ the Jew at prayer could, in one of his favorite, most profound, and most moving prayers, presume that the promise of the "new covenant," including what it says of the new heart, was fulfilled. As a sinner he was excluded from the community of those who proclaimed God's praise in community worship. When he prayed to God for the gifts he needed to enter again into this community, then he could ask that God would create for him what was of the essence of the statement of the promise of the new covenant: a heart renewed interiorly and completely attuned to the recognition of the will of God. God is disposed to the one whom he allows to pray thus.

All this, however, does not exclude that the promise of the "new covenant" was only fulfilled in its definitive, eschatological fullness in Jesus of Nazareth. Nevertheless, it must be acknowledged that this fulfillment did not have its beginning in Jesus. Jer 31 speaks of something that penetrates to the very depths of the heart, granted to a Jewish people which does not yet look into the countenance of its promised messiah.

VIII

Rom 9–11:
The "New Covenant"
for the Entire Israel

THESIS: Rom 11:26–27, with composite citations from Isaiah, speaks of a "new covenant" which awaits an as yet unbelieving Israel. The basis of this hope is the love of God for this people because of the patriarchs. This love God never renounces. It embraces the children of Abraham even in the period of their unbelief.

The most important text in the New Testament about those Jews who, after the coming of Jesus of Nazareth, did not follow him is Rom 9–11. The category of "covenant" appears at the very beginning. The many gifts which God bestowed upon the Jews (not only on those before the time of Jesus) are enumerated, including the "covenants" (9:4). I have already dealt with this passage above.

But what is more important is that the word "covenant" occurs again at the climax of the three chapters. When Paul expresses definitively his conviction of the ultimate "salvation" of the whole of Israel which is to come, he does it again by means of the category "covenant."

However, before I develop this, a warning! We modern Christians who are victims of a reading of the scriptures which is individualistic, spiritualistic, and directed to the beyond must once more give ourselves cause for pause so that we do not read the texts of the Bible entirely incorrectly. It is a question of the word "salvation" and all that is connected with it in Rom 9–11.

It is not a matter of saving the soul from eternal damnation. "Savior" in antiquity was one of the most important titles of kings. People were thoroughly convinced that human society was permanently on the brink of plunging into chaos. It had to be "saved" from this ever imminent demise. The one who guided people in orderly fashion and took care that there was general prosperity in the city or even in a whole empire was a "savior."

The "blessing" too which is to come upon the world is of an earthly kind. God will save and bless all his creatures by initiating his salvation and blessing among a particular people. Rom 9–11 deals with the dramatic moment when God's action bursts the barriers of this people and encompasses all nations. At this moment Paul and his addressees experience that a part of the people from which salvation originates does not allow itself to be taken up into the wave of salvation now spreading across the world. Are they beyond "salvation"? Have they become inexorably "hardened"? Has God released them from the function which was theirs of bringing blessing to the world? Has he "rejected" and "cast them out"? These are the questions that Paul puts—it is not a case of individuals to be hurled into hell after death and to lie there cast out forever.

It will be clear to anyone who reads the examples from the history of Israel which Paul gives in detail in chapter 9 that what is at stake is the role of Israel for this world and its history and nothing else. It is the freedom of God in his choice of the children of the patriarchs through whom he will continue the history of his people. Then it is the rescue of Israel from the oppression of Egypt, the opening of the history of salvation on the nations and the contingency that in Israel not the whole people but only a "remnant" of Israel carries on the task as an instrument of God's action in the world. That the dimensions of "salvation" are the dimensions of this present world becomes clear at the end of Rom 9 in a citation from Isaiah which Paul puts forward:

> for the Lord's sentence on the earth will be summary and final (Rom 9:28; cf. LXX 10:23).

It is a question of *ploutos,* "enrichment of the world" and "enrichment of the nations" (11:12). That is of course an "enrichment" which is the ultimate enrichment by means of God's "splendor" present in the world (9:23).

And so, we must not link any false statements of the question with the important text, Rom 9-11, such as the "predestination" of the individual soul. The crucial question is: What role in God's plan in history will God assign to that part of his people which does not see this crucial new orientation, and so no longer submits itself to his saving action when it is extended anew to the many nations, even though this action is in the interests of this people and takes a form hitherto visible to it? Are they then off-stage? Or is that once more wrapped in God's plan in history so incomprehensible to us?

Paul is seized and stimulated by his exposition. It all stirs him to the depths because his own people is at stake. He is torn this way and that so that he says at the beginning he would almost wish to be "cursed," that is, to be expelled from the community of the holy, to be no longer with Christ from whom God's salvation is now spreading through the nations, but with his brethren who cannot see this (Rom 9:3). So strong is the cry of blood. He uses every sort of mental process and pleading that he possesses, and he uses every faculty to the limit to spare him such consequences. And as the texts of scripture run to their conclusion, the mystery of God's plan in history confronts him (Rom 11:33–36). He senses what is now going on before him and he sees the future already foreseen by God. As the scene unfolds and he reaches the climax of his exposition he once again seizes on the category of "covenant" in a citation from scripture (Rom 11:26–27).

More accurately: He constructs a combination of citations out of two (if not three or four) Old Testament texts, both in the Greek version of the translations available to him, in which the crucial statement is made by means of the word "covenant":

From Zion shall come the Deliverer;
he shall remove wickedness from Jacob.
And this is the covenant I will grant them,
when I take away their sins (Rom 11:26–27).

There is no doubt that a future event is meant, and therefore a future "covenant." How does this citation fit into the former treatment of the word "covenant."

If one wants to demonstrate this, one cannot bypass a rather complicated chain of observations and reflections. But it could be worthwhile. First, we must examine more closely the way in which Paul constructs his scriptural citation. Then we must ask what his intention may have been as he went about it. It will become evident that he really wants to allude to the promise of the "new covenant." But one must then explain why he does not quote directly the text of the "new covenant" from Jer 31. This explains, and only thus does it become quite clear, what Paul really wants to say.

First then: What are the sources from which Paul draws the material of his construct citation? The first half of his constructed text comes from Is 59:20–21, the surprising end of a long chapter full of accusations, acknowledgements of guilt, and threats of divine judgment. The whole world of the nations from east to west will fear "the glorious name of the Lord." "Anger will come from the Lord like a rushing river. He will come with passion." And therein the surprise.

> The savior will come from Zion. He will remove all godlessness from Jacob. And that is the covenant which I have instituted for you, says the Lord (Is 59:20–21 LXX).

Paul appends to this text a passage from what is known as the apocalypse of Isaiah (chapters 24–27). It speaks of the reconciliation of Israel at the end time:

And so the lawlessness of Jacob will be removed,
and this is the blessing for him when I take away his
sins . . . (Is 27:9 LXX).

Paul obviously feels himself justified in joining the concluding temporal clause with Is 59:20–21, even though
by doing so he takes it out of its original context. Why?
First, there is a statement here also about the removal of
Israel's sin. Israel is likewise called "Jacob." Then follows too a clause introduced by "this is." Is 59 reads:
"This is the covenant"; here the text runs: "This is the
blessing." As Gal 3 has shown in regard to the promise
to Abraham, the words "promise," "covenant" and
"blessing" are very close to each other for Paul. Hence
he can append what follows in Is 27:9 to describe the
future blessing to Is 59:21 which describes the future
"covenant."

But why does Paul have recourse to this procedure?
I see only one explanation: he succeeds thereby in alluding at the same time to the oracle of Jeremiah about the
"new covenant." It is there that God promises his people a "new covenant," and it is described at the end:

Because I will pardon their breaches of law, and I
will remember their sins no more (Jer 31:34 LXX).

There is only one other passage in the Old Testament
where an assurance of the forgiveness of sins follows on
the assurance of a future "covenant" in this way. Apart
from Jer 31:31–34, I could name only the passage in Ez
16:59–63 which belongs to the narrow circle of Jer 31:
31–34. It is concerned with a future "everlasting cove-

nant." But the link between the themes "future covenant" and "forgiveness of sins" in the oracle of Jeremiah is very striking. There, the clause about the forgiveness of sins is formulated in two parts and forms the resounding conclusion of the text. In Ez 16, it is the theme of "shame" that is in the foreground and not that of forgiveness. The early Christian tradition of the last supper has also taken up the combination of motifs.

Although he quotes from Isaiah only, Paul, by his combination of citations, succeeds in referring to the Jeremian promise of the "new covenant." The Greek version of Jer 31:34 does not speak of "their sin" (as does the original Hebrew), but of "their sins." Hence Paul was able to change the singular formulation "his sin" in the Greek version available to him of Is 27:9 into the plural formulation "his sins" when he combined the citations. We would then have as well a direct influence of Jer 31 on the text of Rom 11:26-27.

But why did Paul make it so difficult? Why did he not simply quote the oracle about the "new covenant" itself? The simplest explanation would be: because he did not have a Jeremiah scroll with him from which he could verify the text exactly. But that is speculation. There are two further concrete explanations which could have prevented him from quoting Jeremiah directly—as the letter to the Hebrews was to do later without inhibitions. One is: this oracle had in the meantime become so intimately linked with the tradition of the last supper for his Christian readers and would have been taken as already fulfilled in Christian life. Paul would have been afraid of upsetting them by direct citation. He wanted to avoid this. But there is another reason: Paul obviously knew the text from Jeremiah, as he did the whole Old Testament, in its Greek form. The Greek version, however, gives a meaning to a very obscure passage in the Hebrew different from that which I gave above when discussing Jer 31 in agreement with most modern Old Testament scholars. I had translated:

> This covenant of mine they broke, although I was their master (Jer 31:32b).

The old Greek version on the contrary renders the passage thus:

> They did not abide by my covenant, and (so) I cared for them no more.

This statement would not accord at all with what Paul intended. He wants to say that God continues to care even for that part of Israel which does not believe in the promised messiah who has now come. For this reason as well the citation from Jeremiah would have been upsetting. He holds it to be better to create a combination of citations which in its final effect says the same as the passage from Jer 31, but does not contain a disturbing formulation. It will be seen to be probable that Paul was aware of this formulation in the Greek version. So much for the combined citation of Is 59:21 and Is 27:9 which announces in Rom 11:26–27 a covenant for Israel at the end of history. Following on this, Paul must naturally give the reason why this ancient promise of God still holds good even when people from Israel do not believe in the messiah. That part of Israel which has not followed Christ is indeed "disobedient" and has become "God's enemies" by this working of history (11:28).

Paul makes two statements to support this: one, that though the Jews are separated from Christ, nevertheless

> they are his friends because of the patriarchs (Rom 11:28).

The other:

> for the gracious gifts of God and his calling are irrevocable (Rom 11:29).

First, a note to the second statement. Paul says that God's gifts and calling are *ametamelēta,* that is, "never revoked, never revocable." This is to be seen as an allusion to that passage in the Greek version of the Jeremian words about the new covenant which Paul, according to the reflections advanced above, did not find entirely suitable. The same Greek root occurs there. "I cared for them no more" is in Greek: *egō emelēsa autōn.* Paul therefore contradicts, at least for those among his addressees familiar with the Bible, a particular explanation of the oracle of promise from Jeremiah—however, only in the interests of the inner logic of the Pauline text.

The first statement, they are his friends because of the patriarchs, is, to be sure, based on the second, that God never revokes his gifts or callings. But Paul does not give any basis for the second. He has no need to do so for readers who know the God of Israel from the scriptures.

They would remember at once a passage from the book of Hosea. After several chapters in which he demonstrates their guilt and threatens judgment, God says suddenly and quite abruptly (thus turning upside down all that had been said so far):

> How can I give you up, Ephraim,
>   how surrender you, Israel?
> How can I make you like Admah
>   or treat you as Zeboyim?
> My heart is changed within me,
>   my remorse kindles already,
> I will not let loose my fury,
>   I will not turn round and destroy Ephraim;
> for I am God and not a man,
>   the Holy One in your midst.
> I will not come with threats like a roaring lion
>   (Hos 11:8–10a).

Hosea is dealing here with the people of the northern kingdom of Israel who have been sent into exile in Assyria because of breach of the covenant (cf. Hos 8:1). At the time of Jeremiah this was already more than a century in the distant past.

Nevertheless, the same group is the subject of those genuine Jeremian texts which the deuteronomistic redactors have set within the oracle on the "new covenant" in Jer 30–31. The text is as follows, with an obvious link with the words of Hosea just quoted:

> Is Ephraim still my dear son,
>   a child in whom I delight?
> As often as I turn my back on him
>   I still remember him;
>   and so my heart yearns for him,
> I am filled with tenderness toward him (Jer 31:20).

This profound insight of the prophet Jeremiah into the loyalty of God, which outlives all human sin, to those whom he once began to love, became for the revisers of the book of Jeremiah the reason why they ventured to formulate the promise of the "new covenant" for that Israel which in the meantime had lapsed, as a whole, from the "covenant." God cannot act otherwise; he must have mercy on his people. That God never revokes his gift and calling is therefore the basis of the oracle on the future "new covenant" in the book of Jeremiah.

The text on the "new covenant" in Jeremiah is later expanded further by three verses which underscore precisely this point, the irrevocable love of God for his people. They speak of the fixed order of the universe, of the sun, moon, stars, and roaring sea, and continue:

> If this fixed order could vanish out of my sight,
>   says the Lord,
> then the race of Israel too could cease for evermore
>   to be a nation in my sight (Jer 31:36).

We are taken almost automatically by Rom 11:29 back to Jer 31.

The notion that God never takes back what he has granted to someone, or what he has called someone to, has been expressed in other Old Testament contexts, and in combination with the word "covenant" as well.

Besides the "covenant" of God with the whole people of Israel there is also the tradition of the "covenant" of God with David and his dynasty. From Deutero-Isaiah on, both traditions dovetail into each other. The word "covenant" is not yet used in 2 Sam on the occasion of Nathan's promise. However, the question does play a role there, namely what will happen when one of David's successors lapses from God:

> When he does wrong, I will punish him as any father might, and not spare the rod. My love will never be withdrawn from him as I withdrew it from Saul, whom I removed from your faith (2 Sam 7: 14–15).

This is transposed into the language of the covenant in Ps 89:

> If his sons forsake my law,
>   and do not conform to my judgments,
> If they renounce my statutes
>   and do not observe my commands,
> I will furnish their disobedience with the rod
>   and their iniquity with lashes.
> Yet I will not deprive him of my true love
>   nor let my faithfulness prove false;
> I will not renounce my covenant
>   nor change my promised purpose (Ps 89:31–35
>   [30–34]).

The following verses take this thought further. It is twice said that David's dynasty is to last forever.

But with the fall of Jerusalem in 587 the dynasty of David came to an end. At this moment, Is 55:3–5 takes up the tradition of the covenant with David and transfers it so to speak across to a David-covenant with the whole of Israel. At the return from exile, God will assign to the whole of Israel a role among the nations such as David once had for the nations of Canaan. It is in this context that the covenant with David and this "new covenant" are designated together as an "eternal covenant":

I will make a covenant with you, this time for ever,
to love you faithfully as I loved David (Is 55:3).

At the same time the formulation of the "eternal covenant" in the "priestly writing" acquires great significance. This new exilic version of the historical narrative of the Pentateuch has thereby transposed God's "covenant" from Sinai to Abraham because the narrative carries Israel's existence, looking upon it as a reality whose lasting validity is to be in no way conditioned by Israel's conduct. Consequently, it calls God's "covenant" with Abraham an "eternal covenant" as well (Gen 17:7). This means, as the whole course of the historical narrative shows, that Israel can become unfaithful to its God in certain generations and be punished accordingly. But in the next generation God's loyalty to his covenant promise comes to life again and he continues the history of his people. The great paradigm is the generation that sinned after the exodus from Egypt and so must perish in the wilderness. It perishes, but despite this God leads the next generation into the land that he promised to Abraham in Gen 17.

The "priestly writing" takes its origin from the same epoch as the promise of the "new covenant" in the book of Jeremiah. In both cases, the same basic conviction—that God never revokes his gifts and callings—has been expressed with the help of the same idea of "covenant," though in different ways—in the one case by means of the notion of the "eternal covenant" with Abraham which on God's part outlives all Israel's sins, in the

70

other, by means of the notion of the "new covenant" in the distant future beyond the epoch of sin, in which, as a consequence of the irrevocable love of God for his people, the "covenant" of the beginning shines anew and even more brightly.

Together with this typical use by the "priestly writing" of the idea of covenant, another text from Deuteronomy must be considered which likewise has its origin in the same period. In Deut 4 Moses announces the Babylonian exile to the people before they enter the land, portraying their great distress, their remoteness from the God of Israel, and foretells that Israel can look for and find its God again even there. The passage continues:

> When you are in distress and all these things come upon you, you will in days to come turn back to the Lord your God and obey him. The Lord your God is a merciful God; he will never fail you nor destroy you, nor will he forget the covenant guaranteed by oath with your forefathers (Deut 4:30–32).

Gen 17 and Deut 4 can demonstrate how the notion of the loyalty of God to his word once given links up in a particular way with his promise to the patriarchs. It becomes clear here why Rom 11:29 can be the basis of what is said in Rom 11:28, and how everything coheres internally.

However, at the same time be it noted: in Rom 11 Paul did not use the idea of the promise—"covenant" with the fathers, never to be revoked because of human infidelity—but rather relied on the Jeremian idea of the "new covenant" in his combination of citations from the book of Isaiah.

To return to the beginning of this booklet: Pope John Paul II in his formulation of the "old covenant never revoked" relied, from the perspective of biblical language, both correctly and incorrectly on Rom 11:29. Correctly: because here Paul actually takes up the notion of the loyalty of God to the covenant once instituted, as Gen 17 or Deut 4 has developed it and drawn it into the covenant idea itself. Incorrectly: because Paul in this context makes use rather of the idea of a "new covenant" which God, because of his love and in view of the promise to the patriarchs, will only grant in the future. The idea of the "new covenant," within his individual manner of speaking, presupposes that the "old" has been broken on Israel's part. To that extent it no longer exists at the moment when the "new covenant" is promised. Of course nothing follows with regard to God's position because of Israel's attitude. God does not disavow. And the "new" which he finally gives is the "old" shining even more gloriously. And so one can, though not on the basis of biblical linguistic imagery, but on the basis of the reality, propose the following correct formulation: the Jews, who do not accept the message of Jesus, are nevertheless always and for all time "the people of the old covenant which God has never revoked."

But back to Rom 9–11! If we presuppose that Paul at the end of his exposition—with a formula that is deliberately somewhat different—sees the "new covenant" coming for that part of the Jewish people which in the future does not believe in Christ, then this part, according to Paul, is not yet in the "new covenant" when he is writing the letter to the Romans—at least inasmuch as, according to the conviction of early Christianity, Jesus and those believing in him are in it. The Jews who do not

believe in Jesus are loved by God because of the patriarchs, but they are not in the "new covenant." Only
those Jews who have already accepted belief in the
Christ are now in the "new covenant."

They alone are now growing as the real shoot from
the old olive tree on which the wild branches from the
nations have been grafted; the Jews who have not yet
come to faith are the branches that were lopped off;
when they do come to faith and so come into the "new
covenant," they will be grafted onto the tree again by
God. It is only in this way that one can understand without contradiction the image that Paul unfolds in Rom
11:13–24. The Jews who believe and those who do not
believe as well as the pagans who have been grafted on:
all take their strength from one single root, the patriarchs—the pagans by means of the wonder of the graft-
ing. But one can certainly not say that Paul wants the
branches that have been lopped off to remain separated
from the life cycle of the whole tree. God will graft them
in again. The "savior" who comes for them from Zion is
Jesus. From the love of God, never revoked, he brings to
them the "new covenant." If he comes not so much
from heaven but from Zion, that means that for Paul the
true Mount Zion with the true sanctuary is there where
there is belief in Jesus the Christ.

The Hebrew as well as the Greek text of Is 59:20
reads that the savior will come *"for* Zion." Supposing
that there was no other text available to Paul, a text of Is
59:20 not preserved for us, then, perhaps relying on a
key word at the beginning and end of Ps 50 (cf. vv. 5 and
16 and the role of the word "covenant"), he has altered it
himself: because in the combined version the savior
comes *"from* Zion." That would show how important it

was for him that the true "Zion" is now to be sought on the side of the church, not among those Jews who remained outside belief in Jesus.

All these reflections show how much Paul is driven by the conviction that God continues his history with those who believe in Jesus Christ. It is all the more impressive then when he pressures all that he can yet say in favor of a role that is still available for those Jews who do not believe in Jesus.

Naturally, the idea of the "new covenant," as we have rediscovered it in Rom 9–11, is always intended in its eschatological depth which, in the analysis of Jer 31, can only be fulfilled as in Christ. That fulfillment of the prophesying of the "new covenant," which began with the return from Babylon and can take on dimensions as indicated in Ps 51, is not thereby touched. Paul, captivated entirely by the Christ event, does not at all have it in view. In the sense of this not yet definitive eschatological fulfillment, one could naturally say at the same time that the part of the Jewish people which does not believe in Jesus, of whom Paul spoke in all his zeal for the torah, had a share in the "new covenant." But these questions lead us into the next chapter.

IX

Reflections on Rom 9–11 After Two Thousand Years

THESIS: Perhaps we should take a fresh look at Rom 9–11 today. This will presuppose that history is now on a course in which the pagans who were grafted onto the olive tree now run the same danger of betrayal as did previously the members of the chosen people. Has it reached a stage today when the Jews must make the Christians "jealous"?

We may not content ourselves with establishing the exact sense and linguistic usage of a biblical text, especially when it is so situated that we have to read our present situation from it. This is certainly the case with Rom 9–11. There are still "brethren" of Paul who do not believe in Christ and for whose sake he could wish to be "cursed" and separate from Christ. What has the text of Rom 9–11 to say to us today after nearly two thousand years, and how are we to elaborate it further in the circumstances?

We have already discussed all the biblical texts which are important for the question of the covenant in which Israel finds itself. We begin then with something of a general reflection on the current "theological" situation, although I will be concerned mainly with Rom 9–11 as my point of departure.

One thing must be said: the idea of "covenant" that the New Testament takes up above all and renders thought-provoking is the deuteronomistic-Jeremian. The idea of the "eternal covenant" with the patriarchs in the sense of a pure promise is by no means missing. But it is the "covenant" of Sinai where the torah, the social order given by God, belongs that gives cause for thought. God's lasting love for the people he once chose leads him, after Israel has breached the covenant, to promise a "new covenant" which is none other than that which shines still more brightly from Sinai. The New Testament sees the definitive fulfillment of this promise in Jesus Christ.

The following tension now arises from our reckoning with Rom 9–11: as we saw when dealing with Jer 31, the "new covenant" was granted to Israel in its post-exilic period. At the same time, however, according to the conviction of the New Testament, this promise comes to its profound and radical fulfillment only with Jesus the messiah and those who believe in him. As Paul teaches, for those Jews who, after the coming of Jesus, live on through history without attachment to him, but whom we continue to designate as the "Jewish people" today and whom God continues to love, entrance into this "new covenant" in the full sense is still impending.

One must handle the words "old covenant" very carefully in this context. It is perhaps not for nothing that it occurs only once in the whole Bible. But where it does occur, the talk is not of the breach of the covenant of Sinai set out in the book of Jeremiah; rather it is obvious and taken for granted that it is speaking of the Jews at the time of Paul who do not believe in Jesus and are still in the "old covenant." It is a matter of the *one* covenant, formulated from Jer 31, inasmuch as it is once again new through the post-exilic fulfillment. It can only be designated as "*old* covenant" in comparison with the eschatological fulfillment of the Jeremian promise which took place in Christ. There is a definite sense then in which the "old covenant" of 2 Cor 3 is the "new covenant" of the book of Jeremiah. We could say then that the contemporary Jewish people lives in the "old covenant" though this is at the same time now a "new covenant."

If one wanted to put this conceptually, then one would have to distinguish between those who live in the "pre-messianic new covenant" and those who live in the "messianic new covenant." But as soon as one does this, one is ill at ease and would prefer to avoid such talk

This uneasiness is based on the situation itself. It simply cannot be that a promise of God is not completely and universally fulfilled. Paul wrote Rom 9–11 out of an impossible situation under which he suffered severely. He did not formulate it with the help of the idea "covenant." I have formulated it in this way. But it is one and the same situation. And it is still the same today as it was then.

Perhaps we can describe our concern with the aid of an idea which has been developed in sociology, "the simultaneity of the non-simultaneous." Both Jews and followers of Jesus of today live simultaneously; something has already transpired with one group which is still outstanding for the other. This is not a matter of immobility but of a constant struggle. What is non-contemporaneous could become contemporaneous.

Paul seems to have had something like this in mind when he gave his explanation of the situation. According to him a part of Israel—from God's point of view—did not open itself to his messiah in order that salvation might burst upon the other nations. On the other hand, the nations have been drawn into the saving process so that those who do not yet see the messiah may become "jealous" and their hour may come (Rom 11:11). And so there is a struggle in progress between two groups. Nothing is definitive.

Moreover, it is incorrect to work simply with the ideas of "already" and "not yet" in this context. The word "already" carries something positive with us, "not yet" something negative. But that a large part of the Jewish people were "not yet" believing in the messiah was the very reason that the message went over to the nations. The "not yet" then, which from Jewish perspective was and remains a straight-out "not," carries something positive for Paul. And our "already," with its positive echoes, which is valid for the nations, means at the same time that they have been put into much greater danger. This brings something negative to the word. The nations have now to share full responsibility for the salvation and future of the world which hitherto the Jews alone had to bear, and woe to them if they fail.

Paul ultimately gives clear expression to the negative association of this "already" from the more than one thousand years of experience of Israel which hitherto bore sole responsibility for God's history in the world:

Very well: they were lopped off for lack of faith, and by faith you hold your place. Put away your pride, and be on your guard; for if God did not spare the native branches, no more will he spare you. Observe the kindness and severity of God—severity to those who fell away, divine kindness to you, if only you remain within its scope; otherwise you too will be cut off, whereas they, if they do not continue faithless, will be grafted in; for it is within God's power to graft them in again (Rom 11:20–23).

This unmistakable warning anticipates a history of freedom that ranges far and wide. Only at its end will the savior come from Zion for that Israel which has not accepted his Christ and take it into the "new covenant." In the meantime a history is running its course in which those from the nations who have been grafted onto the old olive tree are themselves in danger and through their own fault can fall away from their calling. This forces us, after almost two thousand years of such history, to look back and ask what has happened in the meantime and what may have to be added by way of supplement to the text of Rom 9–11 from Paul's perspective.

The presupposition for such a new reading of Rom 9–11 is that which has been elaborated, especially in the exegesis of Jer 31. The people to whom Jeremiah announced the return as the signal for the renewal of the covenant, and who, to the astonishment of the nations, did return and were able to continue their life down to the present, are not to be regarded just as a group that has become blind. God is likewise effecting in them his "new covenant" promised by Jeremiah. They must be recognized by us Christians today as a sign of God among the nations. They have always been such a sign and remain so precisely in our days. The millions killed in the Shoah are a sign. The return to the land of Israel is a sign. The love of God for the children of Abraham goes further even if he at long last has allowed something new to arise out of their midst in which the oracle of Jeremiah, according to our Christian conviction, proves to be definitively true.

But what in the meantime has come out of this new thing? When a great part of his people did not believe, God used this to set in motion the promise of the pilgrimage of the nations at the end time. But the purpose of the belief of the pagans was, as Paul teaches us, that those Jews who delayed might become "jealous." But how little have the nations who were drawn into the process of salvation remained faithful to their task—and it is to this that I now come. Is Christianity today anywhere near that stage that could make the Jews "jealous"? Where is it obvious that it is removed from the sinful and lethal structures of the world and that the glory of God is in its midst?

Paul could not have known that it would come to such a darkening of the faith of the nations. Has not the situation which he describes in Rom 9–11 been reversed? Those who believe in Jesus as God's messiah have forgotten what God's gift looks like and what they are called to. They must be urged to recognize anew "the Jewishness in Christianity" as I have formulated it in the title of my book mentioned in the Foreword—the "Jewishness," because perhaps today Jews are in many ways more aware of the "covenant" than Christians. In their own way they stand within it just as do Christians.

But Christianity has allowed itself to be assimilated so much to many and ultimately interchangeable religions; in an immensely complicated and world society it has come to see its task almost solely as a concern for individual souls which receive some little experience of the transcendent through ritual communication; they are comforted in distress by hope in the beyond. Perhaps present day Jews are more aware that God will change the world, and so needs a "people," a society, which in contrast to the other societies in the world tries to live according to God's original design for the world. What use is it then to us Christians when we confess Christ in whom the one "covenant" has concentrated itself to eschatological radicalness and so has become the "new covenant" in the ultimate and most profound sense? If only we would open our eyes and would look once more at the Jews to see what "covenant" really means!

What other conclusion can one draw than that Jews for their part must make Christians "jealous" through what they are! And so there is no "already" for Christians and a "not yet" for Jews, but rather a "still" for Jews and a deeply shameful "no more" for Christians. Everything becomes complicated and ultimately imponderable—as does all that is really historical.

We are stuck in the middle. One must be very modest. One loses the desire to appraise. One tries to be grateful for what one has received as a gift and to bewail what one has wasted. One looks to the other to see if one can learn from him again.

I speak as a Christian. But I ask myself whether a real Jew from his point of view shudders in like manner at the unfathomableness of God's ways in history. He reads in his Bible of the once and for all election of his

81

people. He reads at the same time of God's "covenant" with the whole human race after the flood. He reads of the pilgrimage of the nations to Zion which is to take place in days to come. He reads of people from the nations who worship in Jerusalem and associate with the people of Israel. He reads at the same time that his people are to become in a certain way priests and mediators before God for the whole human race. He reads of promise, guilt, and forgiveness. He too can only shudder before the unfathomableness of God's ways. They are ways which God has written right through our freedom and our many-fold guilt. Who knows whither tomorrow?

X

A Single "Covenant" But a Twofold Way to Salvation

THESIS: One ought not speak of two "covenants" or even of several "covenants," but only of the one "covenant." The formulation "a twofold way to salvation" can be supported. But this must be understood "dramatically."

Both Jews and Christians are on the way. God is with both. Both are "in the covenant." It is one and the same "covenant." Yet each has it in a different way. Am I speaking now of a twofold way to salvation?

I come now to comment on the different points of view that are presented in current Jewish-Christian dialogue about Jewish-Christian relations. How does God see them? Is there one single covenant? Are there two covenants, or several? Has God only one single way to salvation for all, is there a twofold way, or are there many?

If one moves on to the level of such theorizing, then one ought, I think, best speak of *one* "covenant." That is certain when one takes one's stand more on the covenant idea of the priestly writing. But it is likewise true when one stands by the deuteronomistic concept which lies behind the promise of the "new covenant" and which has been taken over above all in the New Testament.

The "new covenant" of the book of Jeremiah is the renewal and new institution of the covenant of Sinai. It includes the same torah. The "new covenant" of the New Testament is the eschatological fullness of this "new covenant" which has already begun with the return of the exiles from Babylon; it is in this that contemporaneous Jews also stand who do not believe in Christ.

I lean therefore to a one covenant theory which however embraces Jews and Christians, whatever their differences in the one covenant, and that means Jews and Christians of today. This is "ecumenism" at its most basic, to introduce the word so often used today. One is thus very close to the biblical view, for all the variety of biblical language, especially in the matter of "covenant."

I would react differently when it is a question of the image of the "way." From early Christian times Jews and Christians have been on two ways. Because the two ways run their course within the one covenant which makes God's salvation present in the world, I think that one must speak of a "twofold way to salvation."

In any case, one must use such forms of speech with much reservation and caution. Is it normally understood as it would be from the discussion so far?

I think that I often catch the sound of another approach, one that is much more static. There was once a single way. That was the case of the people of Israel before Jesus. Then the way divided. Both paths diverged from each other. One was the path of the Jews, the other, of the Christians, the path of the pagans. At some stage, when there was sufficient distance between them, they began perhaps to run parallel. And God wanted it thus. Right up to the very end of the world each was to run its own particular way. The sun shines on both ways. Each is a way of salvation. One is the path which God destined for his people chosen of old, the other the path which he destined for other nations, the pagans, and which he mediated by means of the connecting link of Jewish-Christians, a very small group and soon to disappear. Jesus of Nazareth was relevant for the latter. He is the messiah of the pagans. Jews do not need him; they are with the heavenly Father without him.

This may sound very nice, but it is too much like a landscape portrait of the story of salvation. History is not like this, least of all salvation history. Paul does not speak in this way. Whoever explains Rom 9–11 thus is in error.

The Old Testament too, whose view is universal throughout, does not permit Israel and the nations each to maintain such reciprocal contact in the future that it outlines. God has only one plan of salvation, and at the end he will be "one." There is guilt in history. There is freedom. There is repentance and reconciliation. There is dramatic action, and it is there that each person and each action affects all other persons and all other consequent actions. It is only when one understands talk of the twofold way of salvation "dramatically" that it seems to me to be acceptable.

Now a brief glance sideways at another idea so as to make clear what I mean by "dramatic." I take what today is on everyone's lips and what I can likewise only consider theologically legitimate when it is grasped "dramatically": "the option for the poor."

One usually speaks of the "option of the church for the poor." Behind such talk is the conviction of an "option of God for the poor." If this becomes a metaphysical or a static non-historical statement, then it is incorrect. God loves all—not only the poor. And the church too must love all.

Because one sensed that, one began to speak some time ago in Latin America of a "preferential option for the poor" ("opción preferencial por los pobres"). This has something of the meaning: God loves the poor, but in such a way that he does not cease to love all. That is neither flesh nor bone. The force of the words "option for the poor" is lost when one speaks in this way.

One must rather understand the "dramatic" nature of this program. That is: it is not always and in principle so. God does not in principle want us to be poor so that he can love us, nor does he want the poor to remain poor so that he can love them even further. But in a given situation in history, at a particular point in the drama, it is true: God takes his stand on the side of the poor and the oppressed, and he must do so precisely out of love for all and for the sake of the wealth of all his creatures.

It was not always the case as it is now. It does not have to remain so. The words "option for the poor" belong to a particular stage of the drama. It presupposes guilt, freedom, and every aspect of complicated, human history. It has its place as a "dramatic" idea.

Likewise, we Jews and Christians have arrived at a point in the drama of our entangled and guilt-ridden common history which we can now explain as the situation of the "twofold way."

Now that all has taken the course which it has, God

wills this situation as well. It is the form in which his "salvation" is present in the world. But he wants this situation to be a "drama": progress in history, forward through change.

There is so much pain, guilt, and anguish that hold the praise of God confined in his creation that the drama must go on. Christians must stimulate Jews to jealousy and Jews Christians.

The image of the two "ways" arouses something too clear and too taken-for-granted in the land of the thousand freeways. What I mean is that we would need at least some other images to communicate again the shock of the historical.

Following the imagery of the Old Testament, God's people is for him his beloved bride. Perhaps we ought simply put the question: Will God be polygamous? Will he have two brides? The answer to this question (rhetorically stated) cannot appear to us as it appeared to our ancestors on the portals of the gothic cathedrals: here, the proud woman, the "church," there, the collapsing, rejected woman, the "synagogue," blindfolded, even though still bearing the beauty and dignity that belong to her.

These portals present the two sides of the historical reality. It shatters us because it is less abstract: not two ways, but two women. But these figures on the cathedral portal betray that the "dramatic" character of the experience is sacrificed. The purely transitory situation of the dualism is fixed in stone and proclaimed as everlasting— to the detriment of one of the women, the rejected one. And so the two women of Strasbourg take their place rightly in the "Museum of the Diaspora" in Tel Aviv as a silent commentary witnessing to the annihilation of the

Jews in our country. They document a static and hence false view of the duality, rightly acknowledged, before us in fact.

The theory of the twofold way will indeed avoid the error of the cathedral portal. Though it certainly avoids only the rejection of the one woman, it does not without more ado avoid the unhistorical character of the image. It arrives at patient resignation before the duality. It does not thereby take the question of salvation in full, this-worldly, historical seriousness, even though it speaks of ways of salvation.

XI

"Covenant" and Eternal Salvation

THESIS: The question of the "covenant" is surrendered the moment that one confuses it with or reduces it to the question of eternal salvation or damnation.

Catholics are particularly prone to accommodate the theological relationship to Judaism within the context in which the Second Vatican Council learned to speak positively of non-Christian religions. All religions are acknowledged there as genuine ways to salvation for their believers at any time. Did not Karl Rahner with his theory of "anonymous Christianity" make this theologically plausible as well? And are there not theologians— and they have not been contradicted—who say that in a certain sense the many religions of the world are the "ordinary" way to salvation, while Christianity itself (we could accommodate Judaism here as well) is, so to speak, the "extraordinary" way?

On this basis, should one not speak of the "many ways of salvation" and perhaps too even of the "many covenants"? In addition to God's "covenant" with the

Jews and his "covenant" with the Christians, there would be also God's "covenants" with other communities of religion.

Occasionally one has recourse to a biblical context for such talk, and one thinks of the covenant with Noah. Could not this indicate the covenantal character of all religions of the human race? Whether this is possible, or not will not be discussed explicitly here. I would point out at most that in the priestly historical narrative, to the language of which the covenant with Noah belongs, the cult was only founded on Sinai. The covenant with Noah is directed only to the preservation of creation. That which constitutes the core of a religion, worship, is not included in the covenant with Noah.

If one stays with the image of the "way" and looks at it "dramatically," then this way of speaking, namely of several ways to salvation, seems to admit of an acceptable sense. The image, if it is to be biblical, must at some time or other flow into the prophetic vision of the pilgrimage of the nations to the hill of Zion at the end time:

> In days to come
> The mountain of the Lord's house
>> shall be set over all other mountains,
>> lifted high above the hills.
> All the nations shall come streaming to it,
>> and many peoples shall come and say,
> "Come, let us climb up onto the mountain of the Lord,
>> to the house of the God of Jacob,
> That he may teach us his ways
>> and we may walk in his paths."
> For instruction issues from Zion,
>> and out of Jerusalem comes the word of the Lord
>> (Is 2:2-3).

The reply of God's people to this message is to call on itself to take the way that God has already given to his people in suchwise that the nations will be encouraged to make their way to Zion:

> O people of Jacob, come,
>   let us walk in the light of the Lord (Is 2:5).

The promise of the pilgrimage of the nations at the end time remains the image which directs the thoughts in the background of Rom 9–11. When Paul speaks there of the "wealth of the nations" and the "wealth of glory," it is the language of the pilgrimage of the nations in Isaiah that is sounding through.

A teaching about the many ways belongs very much to the context about which our reflections circle. All human ways can lead only to Zion, and so they must really be ways of salvation.

Normally, however, statements about the many ways of salvation are not put into such contexts. It seems to me that one often makes a detour to a level, however legitimate within an overall theology, with which one should not proceed when it is a matter of Jews and Christians.

When the Second Vatican Council dealt with the non-Christian religions, the question finally drove the bishops to ask if in fact, as earlier generations of Christians had believed, those who did not make the Christian profession of faith were condemned to hell after death. It was a pressing matter and had to be explained. But is that the real question between Christians and Jews—who after death goes to heaven and who does not? Should this question be taken up when Jews and Christians speak of the way to salvation?

God's everlasting love in the beyond certainly does not fail any persons who ultimately seek him and follow their conscience. And more, every person has the possibility of fresh repentance before God in this life. God's grace pursues everyone, pagan, Jew, or Christian. Whoever is neither Jew nor Christian confronts this grace in the religious institutions in which he or she has grown up. The Old Testament was aware of this. All of us need this grace ever and anew, and it will not be denied us, so we trust.

But I think that within the perspectives of this question, it would be almost a waste of time to formulate further particular theories about the relationship of Judaism to Christianity. Why then continue to speak of two ways of salvation? One must speak at once of endless ways of salvation. And it would be no bad thing were Lessing's Nathan correct with his parable of the ring

But when it comes to Jews and Christians—as was discussed above in Rom 9–11 on the occasion of the key word "rescue" (salvation)—it cannot be a matter of this idea of "salvation." What it means is obvious and always connotated in the word itself. Nothing is to be denied here. It is a question here of the Bible, both Old and New Testaments, when very different words are used to develop the notion of salvation, not only of the salvation of the individual soul, but of the shape of the world which is not in order and which God wants to save.

It is a question of whether and how God changes human history, so characterized by guilt, duality, and power back to what he really had in mind when creating. It is a question of whether unanimous songs of praise can echo again in the desecrated and hollow realms of this world and give glory to God. That at least is the biblical form of the question of salvation. It is a question of heaven and hell here according to the story of salvation.

When one speaks of salvation in this way, Jews and Christians find themselves on one side, while on the other side the world of other religions is not entirely in the same position. God puts into effect the "salvation"-history which he has set in motion by creating a "people" for himself. This is "election." We Jews and Christians may consider it something of a burden to be "chosen." But we must not run away from it by introducing an idea of salvation directed purely into the beyond and be satisfied with it.

One cannot remain indifferent when faced with this tentative specification of the question of salvation when the bearers and protagonists of God's one salvation are divided. They are divided in fact, and so there is now a twofold way to salvation.

If this is so, one must speak of a "twofold way to salvation" in such a way that the one does not deny to the other that it is God's instrument. But to condemn the two ways, facts that they are, to permanent parallelism for all time on the ground that there are simply countless ways to salvation would be to despair of the possibility of the actual salvation of this world, of that salvation of which the Bible speaks. This ends up, hard as it sounds, in unbelief before God's biblical word.

XII

"Covenant" and "Torah"

THESIS: Much would be gained for Christian-Jewish dialogue if, when facing Jer 31 and the "new covenant" of the writings of the New Testament, less attention were paid to the word "covenant" and more to the word "torah."

Perhaps we should return here once more to the text of Jeremiah on the "new covenant." The real theme there is the "torah."

When current Jewish-Christian dialogue speaks of the "twofold way of salvation," one hears again and again the word "covenant," and frequently the word "election." One speaks of the "lasting covenant" of the "lasting election." The words often take on the sound of empty clichés.

In contrast, it would be useful to attend more to the word "torah." Torah: "law," the "law of Sinai." It might be formulated more loosely: the new order in society which God bestowed on his people when he freed them from the oppression and forced submission of Egyptian society. Jer 31 is concerned with this torah.

According to this text, the torah was the same in the former, broken covenant as it is to be in the covenant

94

that is to result anew from God's pardon. It must be the determining factor in it when it enters into its fullness with the coming of the messiah. This, according to Jer 31:33, constitutes the "new covenant": "I will set my torah within them and write it on their hearts." We have already established this in the course of this booklet. But at the end, I would like to underscore it again.

Details in the shape of the torah may change. In the period of ancient Israel they were subject constantly to new formulation. The "legal collections" gathered in the Pentateuch, stemming from different periods, attest to this. Even when confronted with the central text, the decalogue, Israel's freedom to reformulate did not stop. In order that the same might remain so for God's will in regard to the societal shape of his people, it had always to be rethought. Later, orthodox Judaism of the diaspora often adhered to the form of the torah written down in the biblical texts to the extent of holy absurdity and literalness, by every sort of casuistic adaptation to new circumstances; and we can only admire it for this. But there can well be other forms of loyalty to the torah, even though every Jew may not agree with me in this. But one thing holds always: that dimension of the torah that covers "God's people" must remain, its alternative character standing over against those models of society of a world that has fallen away from the original design of creation.

Because of the treatment of the Pauline teaching on law and gospel—often horribly wrong—by Christian theologians, the impression has arisen in normal Christian consciousness that Christianity is just the opposite of what is meant by torah. This was of course quite amenable to all those prone to make out of Christianity something that concerns the individual, the interior life, and ultimately only the beyond.

However, the sermon on the mount is meant to be nothing else than the ultimate interpretation and radicalization of the torah of Mount Sinai. It is not intended to be a substitute by means of another torah, not to speak of it as the negation of torah.

Torah is salvation in concrete form, its materialization, its penetration into the density of society with all that it means. Because torah in the "new covenant" is the same as in the covenant of the exodus from Egypt, it can, so far as it is present in our world in two ways, ultimately be only one torah, God's world confronting the world societies structured out of sin, even if that world stemming from God's torah has to be as rich and varied as can possibly be devised.

What this might entail concretely must be the subject of a new book, or even of several new books. As for Jewish-Christian dialogue, I think that it is much more sensible to strike an attitude to the torah and its thinking than to the idea of "covenant."

When one looks more closely, it is the Christians who have introduced talk of "covenant" into this dialogue. The idea of "covenant" exists obviously for Jews as well. If then reflection on "covenant" in the Bible has as it were led spontaneously to "torah" as perhaps the more central and more existential idea, why not make it the guiding idea of the dialogue? Perhaps then the Jewish partners would not be quite so silent as they are often forced to be at present. And perhaps we Christians would have many an opportunity for ready hearing.